C000197877

Jesus is Dread

Jesus is Dread

Black Theology and Black Culture in Britain

ROBERT BECKFORD

DARTON·LONGMAN+TODD

First published in 1998 by
Darton, Longman and Todd, Ltd
1 Spencer Court
140–142 Wandsworth High Street
London SW18 4JJ

© 1998 Robert Beckford

The right of Robert Beckford to be identified as the Author
of this work has been asserted in accordance with the
Copyright, Designs and Patents Act 1988.

ISBN 0–232–52241–3

A catalogue record for this book is available from the British Library.

The Scripture quotations used are, unless otherwise indicated, from the
Revised Standard Version of the Bible.

Phototypeset by Intype London Ltd
Printed and bound in Great Britain by
Redwood Books, Trowbridge, Wiltshire

This book is dedicated to Deirdre Simpson

Contents

Illustrations

(Between pages 148 and 149)

Lion of Judah by Robert Lentz (1988)
The Last Supper I by Faisal Abduallah (1995)
The Last Supper II by Faisal Abduallah (1995)
Da Resurrection by Faisal Abduallah (1995)

Acknowledgements

On numerous occasions, students, colleagues and church people have asked me to suggest books that articulate Black British approaches to Black theology. I have not been able to recommend much, apart from a limited number of articles and smaller publications. This book was written in response to this situation, to give expression to the emergence of Black theological thought in Britain. However, it is not offered as a systematic treatment of the subject, nor as a defining work. Instead it is a *loose* collection of essays concerned with the interface of Black theology and Black expressive cultures in Britain. I hope that a more specific critical engagement of Black theology will emerge in my PhD thesis, *Dread Pentecostal Theology*.

It was important to me that this book was accessible to people outside traditional academic circles. Consequently, these essays weave together Black vernacular, personal experience and intellectual thought in order to bridge the gulf between Church and academic world. I hope that this book will stimulate discussion and critical dialogue between these those who sit in the pews, preach from the pulpit and teach in seminaries.

This book, although the product of my concerns and interests, could not have been completed without the assistance and support of many individuals. I thank my friend and colleague Dr Randal Bailey for his intellectual support, pastoral guidance and radical pedagogy. Without his unceasing enthusiasm for liberation, I would not have had the self-belief necessary to put pen to paper. Alison Webster helped me with the mechanics of writing this book. In particular she schooled me in the process of publishing. I greatly appreciate the time, enthusiasm and critique that she offered me in this venture. The Black students at Queen's College, and the Black theology support group in Birmingham, provided me with a context for reading and discussing the chapters of this book. Their critique enabled me to reformulate my ideas. Yvette Hutchinson and Mary-Anne Ebert read the full manuscript and provided helpful suggestions and comments. Finally, I would like to thank Trinity Fellowship, Handsworth, for their spiritual empowerment and unconditional love, both of which were invaluable resources for the writing of this book.

Thanks are also due to the following for permission to reproduce extracts from copyright sources.

Bob Marley lyrics reproduced by kind permission of Blue Mountain Music/Bob Marley Music Inc.

Independent Intravenshan, words and music by Linton Kwesi Johnson. Copyright © 1979 L.K.J. Music Publishing Ltd Blue Mountain Music Ltd, 47 British Grove, London W4. Used by permission of Music Sales Ltd. All rights reserved. International Copyright Secured.

Introduction

Press along, saints

> Press along, saints, press along
> In God's own way
> Press along, saints, press along
> In God's own way
> Persecution we must face
> Trials and crosses in our way
> But the hotter the battle
> The sweeter the victory.
> (Black British church chorus)

I am a Black Pentecostal Christian in Britain today *and* seriously concerned with Black liberation. Whereas for many of my parents' generation, Christianity and Black politics were two separate realities, for me they are inseparable. Nowhere was the dichotomy between politics and religion more apparent for many of my parents' generation than in their dislike of Rastafari. Many of my parents' generation considered Rasta politics 'anti-Christian' and 'rebellious', and Rastas 'dirty'.

However, among many second and third generation Black Pentecostalists today, the relationship between Black Christianity and Black politics is clear. This is because Black politics is no longer viewed as (in the words of my parent's generation), 'the cares of the world', or 'taking your eyes off Jesus'. Instead, many young Black Pentecostalists now feel that it is *impossible* to be Black and Christian without

being explicitly political – that is, being actively engaged
with the transformation of the social and political world.

Various social forces have become sources of inspiration
for this new generation. First, Black nationalism in the USA
and South Africa has made Black Pentecostalists in Britain
aware of the global struggle for a full Black humanity. TV
images, newspaper articles and popular songs revealing the
radical action of Black Christians and Black Churches in
the USA and South Africa, have led young Black Christians
in Britain to question their own political role in Black
communities which are besieged by similar forces of racial
oppression. Today, such is the interest in relating Black
religion to Black politics, that in Britain, Black theology is
taught at a variety of levels – including access, undergraduate
and postgraduate – to cater for this new breed of Black
Christian. Second, this new generation has been spurred on
by what it perceives as the failure of the majority of Black
Churches to address political issues in the past and the
present. As a sign of this failure the new generation points
to the many young Black people in the 1970s and 1980s
who found comfort, direction and wholeness in Rastafari
and other Black religious and political groups. Furthermore,
in the eyes of this new generation, the lessons of the past
have not been learned: Black Churches are still viewed by
many within the Black community as escapist and other-
worldly, and therefore an opiate for Black people.

However, the search by new generations of Black Christians for a Black political Gospel raises two important
questions: What sort of method should a Black political
Gospel use? And what should be some of its central concerns? These two questions are the central focus of this
book. In sum, I have attempted to outline the framework for
a Black political theology which prioritises Black expressive
cultures. This approach is contextual in so far as it emerges

from my concerns as a Black Pentecostalist theological educator and Black male in Britain. Furthermore, this approach is a challenge to Black Christians to begin to consider alternative routes for Black Christian theology. In the remainder of this introduction, I want to outline what is meant by a Black political theology that prioritises Black culture. To evaluate this theological perspective, we must explore the three main ingredients:

- Black Christian
- Political theology
- Black expressive cultures.

Black Christian

I want to show first, that Black Christians are diverse; secondly, that we cannot depend upon traditional Western thought for doing theology; thirdly, that Black Pentecostalism can be a focus for exploring a Black theology of liberation for Black Christians in Britain – because its origins and development are complex and dynamic.

1 The diversity of Black Christians

Black Churches are diverse in their origins. Consequently, discussing Black Christianity is challenging because it is impossible to talk about 'the Black Church' as a singular experience or reality. Although there is continuity and commonality within Black experience, it is also important to

acknowledge difference. We are not all the same.[1] Hence,
Black Christian theologies in Britain exist in a variety of
forms. There are Black Pentecostalists who are trinitarian in
belief, as well as Black Pentecostalists who are Oneness (or
'Jesus only') in orientation. There are also Black Sabbatarians
who advocate the keeping of the sabbath. Outside these
Black-led circles there are Black Anglican, Methodist,
Baptist and Reformed Church members within predomi-
nately White denominations – as well as Black Christians
in evangelical and independent house-church movements.
We must also remember the emergence of Asian Christian
traditions and indigenous African Churches in Britain,
which signify increased diversity. Furthermore, when we
consider gender perspectives such as womanism, issues of
sexuality, and the emergence of Black middle-class Christians, we engage other levels of diversity. We might conclude:
Black Christianity is multiple, and negotiated differently in
each location where Black people worship God.

2 The inadequacy of Western models

Black Christian theological thought is difficult to express
using traditional Western categories. This is because, in most
White-led denominations, professional theologians, primarily White, male and elitist, 'do theology' on behalf of
their Churches. In the main, they use methods, concepts
and resources which have emerged from European history,
thought and experience. With few exceptions, White theologians are validated by White-run academic institutions
which maintain British, European and Western scholarly
norms. I am not suggesting that all Eurocentric tools are
similar, or that Eurocentric tools should be understood as a

whole. However, I am suggesting that Eurocentric theological tools are grounded in general premises which are deeply problematic when applied to Black contexts. The Eurocentric tools of analysis that are found in British academic theology cannot satisfactorily evaluate Black Christian theologies, for two reasons.

First, in many cases Black Christian theology in Britain is embedded in the cultural and oral traditions of Black Churches. In these Churches, theology is not some abstract intellectual subject: it is the daily outworking of your 'walk' and 'talk' with God. Likewise, knowing God does not depend solely upon your intellect, but on your immersion in the realm of the Spirit. Although Black Churches recognise the importance of academia and book-learning, they also emphasise a wisdom tradition which comes from meeting Jesus in the worship and prayer of the local church.

The second reason for the inability of Eurocentric theological tools successfully to evaluate the Black Churches in Britain is ignorance. The White academic establishment's monopoly in defining, doing and validating theology in Britain renders Black Christianity and its theologies invisible. For example, despite the emergence, proliferation and establishment of thousands of Black Churches in Britain, Black Christian traditions are still excluded from academic and ecumenical discussions. As a Black Roman Catholic reminded me recently, many White Christians still insist that Black Churches are an aberration in Britain's Church landscape. In sum, we Black Christians who are concerned with a Black liberation theology cannot depend on White academic theologians to do theology on our behalf, or even to consider our interests.

This declaration of independence raises questions for theologians such as me who work in 'the master's theological house' – that is, White theological institutions. On the one hand, we must make use of the resources which we have been able to wrestle away from the White academic power-structures. On the other hand, we must be selective about the tools which we make use of – Black theologians must ask whether these ideas, methods and concepts are really going to benefit Black people. Another way of looking at this issue is to remember the words of Audre Lorde: 'The master's tools *will never* dismantle the master's house'.[2] Therefore, we have to find new tools to do theology on behalf of Black British men and women.

3   The role of Black Pentecostalism

I am convinced that Black Pentecostalism can be a vehicle through which a Black political theology is articulated. While not the only voice, it can be a significant voice. So although this book is written for a wider Black Christian audience, my primary concern is to develop an approach to theology whose starting-point is Black Pentecostalism. There are two reasons for proceeding in this way. First, Black Pentecostalists represent the largest, and possibly most influential, Black British Christian force. No other Black Christian institution has been as successful at mobilising Black people in Britain. As the largest Christian tradition within the Black community, they have built more churches and developed more church-based projects than any other Black church movement in Britain.[3] Second, the similarities between Black Pentecostalism and other Black Christian traditions mean that the hallmarks of the former are not confined to the boundaries of Black Pentecostal churches – rather, they are reflected in a variety of contexts outside Black Pentecostalism. Consider the influence of Black

Pentecostal music and worship-style on the multi-denominational Black choirs. Similarly, many Black Anglicans and Methodists still attend Pentecostal churches in the evening, having been to Anglican or Methodist services in the morning. In other words, I am suggesting here that Black Pentecostalism is more than a denomination or a set of creeds: it is a transcendent and distinctive form of Black Christian experience.

Black British Pentecostalism has complex origins. Black migrants from the Caribbean in the 1950s and 1960s brought with them unique Christian traditions which were the products of:

1. the fusion between African and European religions during slavery;
2. the importation of Black American Pentecostalism to the Caribbean.

Enslaved Africans brought powerful religious and cultural traditions to the Caribbean plantations. Although African traditional religions cannot be described as one homogenous system, as John Mbiti has shown, there are at least four general characteristics common to most African religious systems.[4] These elements of African religions flourished in a variety of hybrid forms submerged within slave Christianity. Such adaptation was possible because African religions remained relatively unchecked by missionary activity – for example, in Jamaica there was no missionary activity from White European missionaries for almost 150 years into plantation history.[5] Albert J. Raboteau summarises the dynamic process of adaptation of African retentions in the New World:

It is important to realise, however, that in the Americas

the religions of Africa have not been merely preserved as static 'Africanisms' or as archaic 'retentions' . . . African styles of worship, forms of rituals, systems of belief, and fundamental perspectives have remained vital on this side of the Atlantic, not because they were preserved in a 'pure' orthodoxy but because they were transformed. Adaptability, based upon respect for spiritual power wherever it originated, accounted for the openness of African religions to syncretism with other religious traditions and for the continuity of a distinctively African religious consciousness.[6]

Slave Christianity was a powerful force for rebellion. In Jamaica, religious leaders led many of the most significant slave revolts. Consequently, the plantation owners, in collusion with willing churchmen, attempted to construct a version of Christianity for slave consumption, which would render slaves obedient and passive. This corrupt form of Christianity became know as the slavemaster's religion, and was diametrically opposed to some forms of Christianity developed by slaves:

In spite of missionary attempts to demythologise the perceptions of slaves, literacy brought them into contact with the world of the Bible which, like their own, was concerned with the relationship between the spiritual and the natural. The biblical accounts of miracles, healings, exorcisms, spiritual power and the presence of the Holy Spirit in people's lives did not seem so different from their own experiential ancestral religion. Furthermore, their identification with the story of Israel's bondage in Egypt and their subsequent Exodus to the Promised Land meant that freedom was understood as more than liberation from the power and consequences of personal sin. An African concept of sin as antisocial activities was reflected in an understanding of the work of the devil as predominantly in the concrete realities of enslavement. The Lord of Hosts who delivered his people from Pharaoh's oppression was the God of liberation from political and social evil.[7]

Finally, it is also important to note that some African religious traditions – for example, Shango in Trinidad, Obeah in Jamaica, Santeria in Cuba and Voodoo in Haiti – were not syncretised with Christianity but remained relatively intact outside the influence of White missionaries.

The second inheritance that informs Black Pentecostalism in Britain is the Pentecostalism movement in the USA. For many students of Pentecostalism, the birth of Pentecostalism is a Black event beginning with the Black Holiness preacher William J. Seymour.[8] Seymour was born in the American South in 1870. His initial Christian orientation was that of the Black American Church in the South. However, Seymour was keen to be a part of interracial reconciliation, and saw the power of the Spirit as a means to transform segregated American society. Seymour found an acceptable doctrine for reconciliation in the Holiness teaching of speaking in tongues. For Seymour, evidence of the Spirit would break down barriers of race, class and gender, because all would become 'One in Christ'. Combined with his Black American spirituality, the dynamism of speaking in tongues as evidence of Spirit baptism culminated in the birth of the Pentecostal movement in Azusa Street, Los Angeles, in 1906.[9]

Seymour built a multicultural church in Azusa Street where, for several years, the outpouring of the Spirit brought heaven to earth, God to humanity and Spirit to body. Women were encouraged to preach, interracial worship was

practised and missionaries were sent to over 50 nations
worldwide in a period of two years. Many Pentecostal scholars argue that Seymour's spirituality consisted of African
retentions in Negro spirituality in America, combined with
new ideas about the manifestation of the Spirit in tongues.
Hence, for some, Seymour was simply doing what his ancestors had taught him: using every aspect of his being to
praise and worship God through interaction with the Spirit
world.[10]

Unfortunately, White racist Holiness preachers who could
not stomach interracial worship eventually split Seymour's
church. Further racial division by White leaders in the Pentecostal movement in the USA before 1920 led to a
distancing from its Black roots.[11] Both Black and White
American Pentecostal traditions, born at Azusa Street, grew
rapidly and were reconfigured among Caribbean people in
the post-war period, especially among poor rural folk, with
their highly syncretised Christianity. It is this faith-tradition
that many migrants from the Caribbean brought with them
to Britain. Given the travelling power of Black Christianity,
it was inevitable that it would become established once
migrant workers from the Caribbean travelled to Britain.

There are numerous reasons for the establishment of Black
Pentecostal Churches, not all of which can be detailed
here.[12] However, two issues are central to understanding its
emergence. First, the theology of worship was an important
factor. As mentioned above, Black people brought with
them a distinctive form of Christianity: they placed a
premium on a holistic approach to worship, which included
the use of the mind, body and spirit working as one
expressive unit in the worship of God. Hence, dancing in
the Spirit, speaking in tongues, praying in unison, synco-
pated rhythmic clapping and body movements were central
to many Christian traditions in the Caribbean. When the

first generation of Black Christians encountered the static, structured and primarily cerebral forms of worship in England's White Churches, they experienced feelings of strangeness only previously surpassed in their history by their African ancestors encountering the oppressive dictates of the slavemaster's religion. But theological difference was not the only reason.

English Churches were at best paternal and at worst racist in their response to the Black settlers. The vast majority of Britain's White-led Churches, as is still the case today, mirrored the racism of the British state and society. In the 1950s and 1960s, while the British government was moving hell and high water to restrict Black migration from the Caribbean,[13] in a similar fashion, members and ministers of the Anglican, Methodist, Reformed and White Pentecostal Churches moved pews, and protested at the Black presence in their congregations. *An opportunity was missed to welcome the stranger*, because, despite the African elements in their worship and their cultural distinctiveness, many of the first generation of Black Christians were colonial citizens. Many had colonial mentalities: England was their mother country – which they knew more about than their African heritage or neighbouring Caribbean islands. Hence, for a large number, warmth, welcome and acceptance would have been adequate compensation for the exclusive practices inherent in the White Church. In fact, where welcomes were warm and ministers sensitive, Black people generally stayed put.[14]

Political theology

The second ingredient which must be explored to evaluate this book's theological perspective is 'political theology of liberation'. In order to explain this phrase, I will ocus on the two terms, 'politics of liberation' and 'theology'.

1 Politics of liberation

When we talk about a political theology we are concerned with the politics of liberation. Liberation is concerned with representing the interests of oppressed people in theological language and action. When applied to theology, it expresses a desire to know what God is doing about oppression, and what is the role of the Christian in God's liberative work in the world. Liberation is both *internal*, concerned with mental emancipation, as well as *external*, concerned with social justice. For Black Christians in Britain today, liberation is an important issue. The struggle for racial justice in education, housing and the criminal justice system are but a few areas where the lives of Black people are under siege. This life-and-death situation for the majority of Black people cannot be overlooked by the few, such as myself, who by their own ingenuity, through luck or circumstance, have managed to escape the cruder forces of White supremacy that seek to steal, kill and destroy Black people. Black liberation should concern all Black Christians of every class and context. After all, to be Christian is to struggle against oppression. The recognition of the relationship between faith and struggle is recognised in the songs of the Black Church, such as:

No weapon formed against me shall prosper
All those who rise up against me shall fall.
I will not fear what the Devil may bring me
I am a servant of God.

When Black Christians sing this, they are singing about the struggle for justice in the world. Some know that evil is more than a spiritual force, and is represented in structures and systems which demean Black men and women. However, to be concerned with liberation is more than just recognising the work of evil in the world: it is about a radical commitment to work for social justice, and not just being concerned with social welfare.

Many Black Christians fail to make the distinction between social welfare and social justice. The Black Church is a brilliant social-welfare institution. People will look out for you and ensure that you have enough to get by, no matter what your situation. Rarely, however, does the Black Church engage in social justice. Social justice involves more than meeting a need: it is about finding long-term solutions to the problems. A good illustration of this tension between welfare and justice occurred when a Black Christian was arrested and imprisoned for a crime he could not have committed. Many churches in the area raised funds to ensure that the man's family was taken care of. However, no church asked the question, 'Why is the criminal justice system wrongfully imprisoning Black men with impunity?' Being committed to social justice is about asking questions and taking risks, so that we can alter the structures and systems that oppress us. This is the task of a Black Christian politics of liberation.

2 Theology

Theology is essentially God-talk – an attempt to express the meaning of God in the world. However, theology is never value-free or neutral: because it is human, our language, motives and ambitions affect its expression. Quite rightly, Black Pentecostal theology places a strong premium on the power of the Spirit continually breaking into our world. This vital ingredient provides Black Pentecostalism with its ability to see, go and do beyond what is considered 'possible'.[15] As a Black Pentecostalist, I take seriously the importance of Spirit guidance in the development of theology; however, I also want to state that theology reflects human interests. In other words, theology tells us as much about God as it does about the human beings who are writing about God. We can illustrate the partiality of theological language by looking at the way in which men have constructed an image of God that makes sense to men and ignores women. In Black Pentecostal Churches, despite the large percentage of women members, very few words, images or ideas reflect the feminine dimension of the being of God. In other words, very few talk about God as being like a woman or a mother, despite such images existing in the Bible. In a similar fashion, Black people have been excluded from God-talk in Western theological discourse. Such is the White academic domination of theology that it is still possible, in the latter part of the twentieth century, for theological courses concerned with 'history' and 'global issues' to focus exclusively on the accomplishments of European White men! However, similar problems concerning the subjectivity of theological language also emerge in theologies of liberation, including Black theology.

Black theology as an academic tradition began with the

writings of James Cone in the late 1960s. Cone attacked
the White Church and White theology: both were complicit
in the racist oppression of Black people in America. In
opposition, Cone developed a Black theology of liberation
which made the oppressed community the centre of theological discourse. In other words, Black theology was a
theology of liberation because the liberation of the oppressed
was its central concern. However, Cone's Black theology,
on another level, was a Black male theology. Almost
immediately after Cone had published his work, Black
women, a few of them former students, critiqued the sexism
in his work.[16] Taking their cue from Alice Walker's understanding of Black womanhood, they corrected the omission
of Black women in Black theology by developing womanist
theology. Womanists retained their concern for the liberation of the oppressed within the Black community. They
introduced the concept of multidimensional oppression
(arising from race, class and gender) faced by Black women
in America, Africa and also in Britain.

Black culture

This study prioritises Black culture as a theological
resource. This is because in Britain, Black people have been
able to use Black culture as a means of expressing the
concerns of Black existence. Black culture is therefore an
important arena for understanding what it means to be
Black in Britain. This is not a new idea: numerous studies
have identified the significance of Black culture for the
African–Caribbean diaspora in Britain.[17] However, what dis-

tinguishes this study is its use of Black culture as a tool in theological reflection for the Black Church in Britain.

Providing one single definition of 'culture' is impossible, because the term has different meanings which are hotly contested. Raymond Williams has described four contemporary usages of the term, one of which defines culture as, 'the signifying system through which . . . a social order is communicated, reproduced, experienced and explored'.[18] This definition, which will be used in this study, describes culture as a dimension of all institutions, including religious institutions such as Black Pentecostal Churches. Furthermore, the definition suggests that human beings create culture as well as being shaped by it. Now that we have established a useful definition of culture, it is necessary to say something brief about the Black expressive cultures which are the focus of this study.

What do we mean when we talk about Black expressive cultures? First, Black expressive culture is neither homogenous nor monolithic. Hence, the 'Black' component in Black culture is understood here as being diverse and multiple. Black cultures are also dynamic – that is to say, they are constantly undergoing change and producing new forms. This means that when we explore culture it is vital to recognise both the *roots* (origins) and also cultural *routes* (dynamic processes of cultural change).[19] Finally, Black cultures are also ideological in the sense that cultural forms can be used to contest power-relationships. For example, Jamaican reggae has long been associated with attempts by the African diaspora in the Caribbean and Britain to legitimate an alternative social world where Blackness signifies power, freedom and emancipation from White power.[20] However, despite the large number of sociological and anthropological studies on Black popular culture, very few explore or expose the spirituality of Black expressive cultures. One of my central concerns in this book is to show that Black culture contains a prophetic and spiritual dimension.

The spirituality of culture is witnessed in Black worship. Within Black Pentecostal Church cultures, divine activity, the work of the Holy Spirit, is understood to be ever-present in the life and worship of the church. Consequently, cultural activities – such as singing, praying and other acts of devotion – are said to be inspired or anointed. When inspiration is most apparent, Black Pentecostal church members may say, of a song, 'It was really blessed', or of a vocalist, 'S/he has the anointing'. Hence, cultural forms within the Black Church are also understood to have a transcendent quality reflecting an other-worldly presence and power. To deny the spiritual dimension of Black expressive cultures is to ignore the spiritual influence and richness embedded within many Black cultural forms, such as Rastafari and Dread culture. What this book is concerned with is the way in which Black cultural forms can be mobilised so as to enable the development of a Black political theology. It is clear that not everything within Black expressive culture is good and wholesome. Even so, we want to draw from particular forms in order to interrogate and transform Black Christianity. This is the central task of a Black Christian political theology which prioritises Black expressive cultures.

This study is a collection of essays which examine the ways in which the mobilisation of Black expressive cultures provides resources for doing Black theology. Hence Chapters 1 and 2 are concerned with church life — in particular, the need for an insurgent Black theology which mobilises Black Christians to think critically about their faith. Chapter 1, 'Independent intravenshan by the rivers of Babylon: the

Black Church and resistance', is a comparison of two songs of communal resistance and communal celebration. One is by Black dub poet, Linton Kwesi Johnson; the other is Psalm 137. This chapter suggests that both forms have the potential to influence how we perceive the Black Church in Britain – especially the myth that the Black Church should be a passive institution. Chapter 2, 'What kind of freed slaves worship in the slavemaster's Church? Black resistance in White Churches in Britain', concerns the 'Black Church' inside the White-led Churches. Culturally, I am particularly interested in how slave resistance critiques the praxis of these Black Christians.

Chapters 3, 4 and 5 are concerned with cultural representations. Because representations have such a profound influence upon our self-evaluation as Black Christians, it is important to explore the ways in which representation can serve the interests of a Black theology. Chapter 3, 'The Masai have a point: Black male sexual representation and Christology', begins this quest by asking questions about sexual imagery and the Church. In particular I am interested in the ability of icons to challenge received notions of Black sexuality, such as the history of negative racialised images[21] of Black men and women in European history. I suggest that one way in which these images can be countered is by examining a Black, sexually potent icon of Christ by Robert Lentz. In a similar manner, Chapter 4, 'Art and soul: Black Muslim art and Black theology', explores themes of gender, race and empowerment in Christian iconography. Through an analysis of Faisal Abduallah's 'Revelations' exhibition, I outline a representational politics in Christian iconography, showing that his work demonstrates, in part, what could be accomplished if Black Christians appropriated and subverted traditional Christian iconography. Chapter 5, 'Watching you watching me', is a documentation of significant ways in which Black Christian cultures are represented in popular culture. I concentrate on three particular issues which emerged in 1996–7 in order to show that issues of marginalisation and exploitation, as well as skill and celebration, feature in the representation of Black Christian cultures.

The final section of the book is concerned with demonstrating how Black expressive cultures, critically appropriated, can affect the development of a Black theology. Chapters 6, 7, 8 and 9 all explore this process. Chapter 6, 'Jah would never give power to a Baldhead: Bob Marley as a Black liberation theologian', concerns finding a theological method in Black expressive culture. Bob Marley would not be top of most theologians' list as a resource for theology. However, I want to suggest otherwise: Marley has a theological method which can be used by the Black Church in Britain today – in particular, his way of evaluating truth-claims, and also his approach to the Bible. Marley points us towards a God of rhythm, a God who is in tune with the rhythms of Black life. The dialogue between theology and culture is continued in Chapter 7, 'Jesus is Dread: language and Christology'. Here, I argue that cultural theory provides a way in which we can investigate Christology: how the Jesus of history becomes the Christ of faith for Black British men and women. I begin with cultural theory, in particular, analysis of Black diasporan cultures. By focusing on the ideological nature of culture, I make a connection between cultural resistance and Christological language. Because European language is limited in its ability to define Black theological thought and Black life, I make use of the concept of Dread in Black cultures (from Rastafari) in order to find a meaningful way of describing Christ's activity in the world today. Chapter 8, 'Sisters in the house: the emergence and challenge of womanist theology in Britain', concerns the cultural politics of gender – that is, it identifies issues of gender in the dialogue between theology and culture. This chapter catalogues the work in progress by the emerging school of womanist theologians in Britain, and explores the cultural issues within their work and practice – all of which challenges and subverts masculinist approaches to a Black theology. Chapter 9, 'Forgive and forget? A Black Christian political rereading of the Lord's Prayer', is the final example of relating culture to theology. Here, we explore what it means to reread the Bible in response to the concrete experiences of the 'reader', especially if the reader is a Black Christian, politically aware and sensitive to the dynamics of Black expressive cultures. I want to show what kind of interpretation might occur when these perspectives are taken seriously.

In sum, developing a Black political theology which prioritises Black culture is one way in which we can take seriously the struggles of Black people. However, Black life is not just about struggle or resistance; it is also about fulfilment and celebration. This holistic approach to life is articulated in the songs and sayings of the Black Church. One phrase that expresses the holistic approach to life is found in the concept of 'pressing on' or 'press along'. To press along embodies what it means to overcome physical or spiritual 'trials and tribulations'. To press along is to be Christ's servants in the world.

Moreover, to press along is to live in the Spirit, because victory is only assured for those who make the Spirit of God their driving force and inspiration. To press along also reveals assurance of concrete victory in the future. However, the assurance of future hope does not negate participation in the struggle here and now. In a similar vein, I hope that this book, while identifying the struggles of Black people, will also identify the holistic nature of our response to being

Black in Britain. This collection of essays is intended as one of many signposts on the journey for all the new generation of Black saints of God who press along.

PART I

Church cultures of resistance

1 Independent intravenshan by the rivers of Babylon: the Black Church and resistance

Independent Intravenshan

Mek dem gwaan, now it calm
But a wi who haffi really ride di staam...
Wat a cheek dem t'ink wi meek, an wi can't spek up fi
wi self
Wat a cheek dem t'ink wi weak, an wi can't stan up pan
wi feet

But mek dem gwaan, now it calm.
But a wi who haffi really ride di staam...
Di SWP can't set wi free, di IMG can't dhu it fi wi,
di communist pawty, cho, dem too awty-fawty
an di laybahrites dem naw go fite fi wi rites

so mek dem gwaan, now it calm
But a wi who haffi really ride di staam...

di CRE can't set wi free, di TUC can't dhu it fi wi,
an di Liberal Pawty is not very hawty
an di Tory Pawty a noh fi wi pawty

mek dem gwaan, now it calm.
But a wi who haffi really ride di staam...
(Linton Kwesi Johnson – LKJ)

Psalm 137

By the waters of Babylon,
　　there we sat down and wept,
　　when we remembered Zion.
On the willows there
　　we hung up our lyres.
For there our captors
　　required of us songs,
and our tormentors mirth, saying,
　　'Sing us one of the songs of Zion!'
How shall we sing the Lord's song
　　in a foreign land?
If I forget you, O Jerusalem,
　　let my right hand wither!
Let my tongue cleave to the roof of my mouth,
　　if I do not remember you,
if I do not set Jerusalem
　　above my highest joy!

Without a doubt, worshipping in a Black church has kept me sane as a Black person of African–Caribbean descent in Britain. Just singing the songs of worship and praise, accompanied by the rhythm and movement of Black folk, provides me with the necessary strength to keep on keeping on. Song in the Black Church has an incredible power to heal, direct and transform human lives and relationships. The worshipping tradition ensures that the Black Church is one of the only safe spaces where Black identities are celebrated and perpetuated. For many, the Church is a place of affirmation and empowerment.

Whether it's through people speaking in patois, singing and swaying, giving testimonies or weeping and crying, the Church affirms the physical manifestations and emotional

expressions of African–Caribbean people in Britain. Consequently, the Black Church for many continues to be a
place of healing in the midst of profound social change and
continued racialised subordination. The Black Church can
also be a place of empowerment. One of my most vivid
childhood memories is of being quizzed continually, by
Pastor Kirby from Bedford, about my progress in school.
He knew that the system worked against Black children,
and he did his best, as a surrogate parent, to motivate me.
Similarly, other church members found time to nurture
me to ensure that I was kept on the right path. This type
of African-centred communal child-rearing ensured that I
was not the only one who found educational encouragement from within the Church. There are hundreds of others
of the second and third generation who were encouraged
to resist the discrimination in the educational system
through the encouragement of a church brother, sister or
pastor. However, despite the Black Church offering space
for affirmation and empowerment, it can also be a place of
oppression.

Oppression within the Black Church

In recent years Black women scholars have articulated the
ways in which the Black Church has institutionally perpetuated male interests (a subject explored further in Chapter
8).[1] For example, Black women have been the primary
agents of the Church's work, and its largest single group.
Despite this fact, sexual discrimination still persists – women
are under-represented in the leadership of most Black
churches.[2] Despite being willing to ordain women, Black

Christian males have found other ways of maintaining the patriarchal hold of the Black Church so that patriarchy is the norm.[3] A common example of the normalising of patriarchy was recently displayed on 'Soul Stirrings', the Black Christian page of *The Voice* newspaper. Marcia Dixon, a female journalist and Black Pentecostalist, listed the ten most influential people in the Black Church: the list consisted of nine men and one woman![4] The piece inferred that there were no influential women within the Black Churches. Similarly, it identified male domination of these institutions, despite the overwhelming numerical strength and spiritual devotion of Black women. Such patriarchal presuppositions suggest that sexism is still a major issue. Interestingly, while Black men have been happy and willing to explore the dynamics of racism, we have rarely spent sufficient time exploring and exorcising the flagrant sexism within our thinking and doing. In fact, many Black male Christians still use the Bible to maintain male hegemony. This happens despite Black Church history telling another story – namely, that God has worked primarily through Black women to build, sustain and empower the Black Church in Britain. Any Church serious about being an alternative community must take seriously the persistence of sexism.

Class discrimination is also another area of oppression within Black churches. Black churches are generally places of social and economic development – if not materially, then at least in terms of aspirations. If you are on the inside, the Black Protestant work ethic will ensure that you have every chance of progression in your personal, social and employment life. Consequently, many Black churches have become hang-outs for an aspiring, Black middle class. According to one Black church-watcher, while some are born into the Church, many middle-class Blacks go to church after 'making it', in order to find spiritual fulfilment.

In its best forms, the aspiring Black middle class is a socially conscious, politically aware group of people who are actively involved in bettering Black social contexts. They are the kind of 'organic intellectuals' spoken of by Cornel West.[5] At its worst, the aspiring Black middle class in the Black Church breaks connections with the Black masses, adopting prosperity doctrines to justify their status and augment the conservative behavioural outlook of the Church.[6] The challenge of the aspiring Black middle class is to maintain the organic connection with working-class and working poor Black people. In other words, the Church must be an institution which empowers the economically marginalised in society.

Another area of oppression concerns sexuality. The vast majority of Black Churches have very rigid and set views on human sexuality. Heterosexism is deemed the only normative sexual expression for humanity; consequently, gay and lesbian lifestyles are strictly prohibited and demonised. In this instance, most, if not all, Black churches are not welcoming places. What concerns me here is not the 'right' of the Black Church to hold its theological position (although there are serious critical issues to debate), but the social consequences of its anti-gay polemic. By endorsing a particular view on homosexuality, the Church also opens itself to the sin of homophobia – the persecution of gays and lesbians. While most Black denominations believe that the Bible is against homosexuality, no Christian can endorse the physical and psychological brutality which is an intrinsic part of homophobia. Any church that calls itself a 'house of God', or more specifically, 'the Church of God', must be a place which all can enter to find solace, guidance and empowerment. If gays and lesbians cannot even gain access because of fear, then the Church has no right to call itself a 'place for the wounded' or a 'shelter in the time of storm'.

Finally, while this concern is primarily articulated in White mainstream Churches,[7] the oppression of disabled people is an issue for Black Churches. Many Black Churches fail to see the wholeness of God in disabled people: consequently, prayer for healing is the only response to disability. On many occasions, I have watched and participated in prayer for healing – moreover, I have had church folk pray for my physical healing. While we must applaud the way in which Black Churches retain a belief in and practice of divine healing, we must be critical of their inability to recognise God's wholeness in those with impairments. A disabled person can be whole through the power of God because God's healing power transcends impairment. The numerous biblical references to impairment as a symbol of divine favour support this point.[8] Therefore, there can be as many 'whole' impaired people as there are able-bodied people who lack the 'wholeness' that Christ brings. The overemphasis on divine healing as the only solution to disability and impairment can make the Black Church an oppressive institution.

Spirituality and liberation

How then might the Black Church develop a spirituality that resists and counters oppression? In other words, what kind of understanding of the presence and power of the work of God must we have? One way of exploring resistance in the Black Church is to look anew at the relationship between spirituality and liberation. Spirituality here is understood as the way in which God goes about the process of holistic liberation in this world. Liberation is also God's redemptive work, concerned with every aspect of human existence. The Church must therefore be a place whose very spirituality ensures that it is God's community of resistance.

Where then do we find models for such an understanding of the Church? Well, our songs often provide us with signs and symbols of what is needed for our wholeness at a given point in time. Therefore we might begin by looking for inspiration to the songs of resistance which are part of Black life in Black Britain. Both popular songs as well as songs within the Scriptures are relevant. To this end, I want to show how two 'songs' of resistance, one from Black British experience and the other from the Scriptures, contribute to our understanding of a spirituality of liberation. The first is by Black British dub poet, Linton Kwesi Johnson; the other is the song of remembrance in Psalm 137. Both are reproduced at the beginning of this chapter.

Black culture, Black struggle

Independent Intravenshan by Linton Kwesi Johnson (LKJ) speaks plainly about Black liberation in Britain. LKJ suggests that the locus or region of Black struggle is not within traditional 'space' or 'places'. Traditional party politics is not a 'safe space' in which to articulate or develop a sustained campaign against oppression. Immigration policy proves his point. Students of British history would acknowledge the racialised immigration policies and the anti-Black policies of political parties of both left and right in the post-war period.[9] Therefore, Black folk cannot look to party politics as a safe bet; there are some systems that will not 'set wi free'. Johnson's assertion also resonates with Black Church history. Black Christians have learned that there is a need for independence from White control because they cannot depend upon White Churches to provide them with a safe haven from racism.

To take LKJ seriously on this point means that we must find 'places' and 'space' which show how to 'ride di staam'. In the history of Black theology, finding such a location for Black Church leaders concerned with civil rights meant allying themselves with the Black Power movement. At that time, it was the places and spaces being carved out by Black Power movements which provided direction and inspiration on how to 'ride di staam'.[10] Likewise we must be willing to seek out places, both inside and outside the Church, which offer this opportunity.

A second aspect of LKJ's poem is the critique of the *status quo*. 'Mek dem gwaan' is a dismissal. It bespeaks dislike: you do not say, 'mek dem gwaan', to something that works on your behalf. On the contrary, 'mek dem gwaan', followed by the pejorative communicative gesture of sucking your teeth, is a clear recognition of the failure of a person, thing or group to meet one's needs. Here, then, LKJ encourages us to be constantly vigilant. We must be aware of, in the words of Marvin Gaye, 'what's going on'. This too has implications for a spirituality of liberation. It identifies the importance of analysis, or what we call, in Pentecostal circles, 'being watchful'. Being watchful here is not just an overemphasis on the end-times and waiting for Jesus to return. Instead it means immersing ourselves in the social context so that we are better able to see what is and is not of God. In other words, we are to have a spirituality that realises the importance of our being agents of the Kingdom of God, here and now. That means paying attention to what is happening in the world. This is a serious issue in Black Churches where there is a historical overemphasising of the eschaton, at the expense of analysis and participation in the concrete social world. LKJ encourages us to shift the emphasis, so that we have a spirituality which realises that the Kingdom is 'at hand', here and now, in the concrete existential world.

Finally, the poem indirectly addresses the role of culture. By using patois Johnson informs us that resistance is intimately related to language. That is, we use language to negotiate resistance. By emphasising Black language-style, its creativity and dynamism, Johnson implies that language and communication is an important aspect of empowerment and liberation. This is because Jamaican patois signifies a particular world-view, community orientation and praxis within this context.[11] Finding language that communicates Black liberation is a challenge on many fronts, especially when we consider Black diversity and heterogeneity. As a result, it will never be possible to find a common language embraced by all. Even so, the challenge to find cultural tools to mobilise Black people has implications for the spirituality of liberation.

A spirituality of liberation for the Black Church must be one that is tied to its cultural context. Black expressive cultures are as diverse as they are dynamic – this is their strength. Consequently, there is a rich reservoir of concepts, themes and ideas which are waiting to be used in the struggle for justice. The mobilisation of culture in Black theology occurred in the South African context, where Church leaders made use of cultural resources to empower and affirm African Christian identity.[12] A similar process has occurred in the US context.[13] These examples are in sharp contrast to Black Churches in Britain, many of which still rely on themes, expression and concepts that come straight

out of White American training manuals from their White
American headquarters. What I am suggesting is that we
can find inspiration for critical reflection on our theology
by listening to, and participating in, the struggles of Black
people on the streets, and in their homes and workplaces.
In short, a spirituality of liberation must make use of our
own language and vocabulary to articulate what God is
doing in the world. This is why, in this book, I suggest,
using the vernacular of Black people on the streets, that
Jesus is Dread.

Roots and routes

We turn now to the second song, found in Psalm 137. A
recent exposition by a colleague and friend[14] has helped me
to see issues of resistance in Psalm 137. Traditional expo-
sitions of this psalm often ignore the strands of resistance
running through it – that is, the ways in which the experience of enslavement caused this community-in-exile to
reflect on their resistance in captivity. Three issues emerge
from this text which are significant for a spirituality of
liberation.[15]

First, it reveals an unwillingness to participate in and
validate one's own oppression. Often unconsciously, many
African–Caribbean British people do and say things, and
live their lives, in a way that permits systems of racialised
oppression and discrimination to take place with no
recourse. This happens in a variety of ways in the lives of
Black Christians. Inside Pentecostal Churches, validating our
own oppression can creep subtly into our own lives: take,
for example, the negative colour symbolism which is part
of Black Church tradition – the way we maintain the myth

(perhaps subconsciously) that whiteness is the colour of purity and superiority. In a context in which people have a long history of oppression and continued racialised subordination, there is a certain absurdity in Black Christians singing, 'Lord, make me whiter than snow'! Such internalisation of negative colour symbolism can be self-debasing, as it fails to affirm the positive aspects of darkness found in the Scriptures, and so articulately expounded by Octavius Gaba.[16]

Similarly, inside White mainstream Churches, African–Caribbean British people are asked to engage in liturgies which negatively evaluate Blackness, Black people and Black culture. Nowhere is this more telling than in the songs and hymnody of the Anglican and Methodist Churches. In these Churches, 'real' church music is generally 'White church music'. Cultural racism is the prime cause of this historical trend. Let me explain. Black liturgies are fixed and essentialised in the mainstream psyche as 'loud,' 'crude' and far too 'emotional'. Therefore, they are never used in White suburban churches. The truth is, however, that Black liturgies enter some churches through the back door: much evangelical song-writing draws deeply from Black gospel music – Graham Kendrick's appropriation of Black gospel music is a good example (see Chapter 5). By ignoring Black liturgies, much worship in mainstream Churches fails to gain valuable insight into the healing potential of worship, so crucial in Black worship-traditions. Similarly, the unification of mind, body and soul expressed in Black liturgies has not been mobilised to breathe life into the overtly cerebral focus of many Eurocentric liturgies. Moreover, because their Churches ignore Black liturgies, many Black Anglicans and Methodists are alienated in their worship setting. Some are simply patronised by the occasional rendition of a 'spiritual' or a calypso-based church song from the Caribbean – usually sung in the wrong key and to the wrong beat. This form of cultural racism[17] is usually justified in the name of tradition. In Psalm 137, the request for 'one of the songs of Zion' tells us that a similar event is occurring here: the Israelites are asked to participate in their own oppression by singing a song of their homeland for the mere entertainment of their oppressors. They refuse to participate in this act, which would decontextualise and dehumanise their experience, reducing it to a consumable commodity.

Black church folk know all too well the danger of decontextualising culture until it becomes a consumable item, far removed from the struggle which has shaped it. Think, for example, of the Black choirs constantly asked to perform 'the spirituals', as if the experience within the songs were a consumer commodity for emotional titillation. Or similarly, the White churches which still want to put on Caribbean evenings to get a 'taste' of the Caribbean. It is safer to ask for a choir than to invite a young preacher to provide contemporary resonance for the songs: I am constantly asked by folk in White mainstream churches to recommend good choirs, but never good preachers. Likewise, it's easier to eat Caribbean food than to read the history of English slavery, colonialism and imperialism in the region. Now, I am not saying that White churches shouldn't seek out Black choirs, nor have Caribbean evenings: I am saying that when these are the only aspects of Black life which are investigated by White-dominated congregations, then all who participate leave themselves open to the charge of being patronising.

Regarding a spirituality of liberation, the refusal to condone one's own oppression emphasises the importance of developing a critical approach to the life of the Church. This does not mean that we run down the Church, but that, as part of a faith community, we explore the inherent bias within the traditions that have shaped us. One way of achieving this end is to hear and take seriously every marginalised voice. This is a very difficult task, which in academia we call 're-tooling' – learning new approaches to doing theology. In the Pentecostal Church we call this kind of openness of heart and mind, 'renewal'. Hearing every marginalised voice can provide insight into how Church systems and structures often encourage us to condone oppression. A spirituality of liberation must ensure that our eyes are open, to guard against the threat of unwittingly validating our own oppression.

The second issue which emerges from the song of resistance in Psalm 137 is the practice of reflection on the past: here, the past is remembered and reflected upon in order to make sense of the present. The past and present have a dialogic role in Black British Church history. We have to take seriously the assertions that diasporan people have to remember the *root*, Africa, but also the *route* or journey that has shaped our experiences. Mobilising our history is not therefore simply a return to all things African: it also involves taking seriously our intersection with European and North American cultures. This kind of cultural hybridity is reflected in Black British church music. At my church, the musical accompaniment to songs ranges from soul to rock, and from reggae to classical. All of these traditions have become part of our multiple and hybrid Christian experience.

Regarding the development of a spirituality of liberation, this second point bespeaks the importance of our knowing who we are. Despite the importance of this matter, the Church is one of the few places where Black history in general, and Black Church history specifically, are undervalued. The ignorance is not due to a lack of appetite for the information, but primarily due to a lack of prioritising. Many churches would rather their young people learn about

the Bible or European Church history than investigate their
own past. The problem here is a common one among
subordinated people: the devaluating of our heritage is perpetuated in such a way that it becomes part of our heritage!
A spirituality of liberation must therefore take seriously the
need for us to be in critical dialogue with our histories.

The final issue to emerge from Psalm 137 is that the
reflection on the past has a particular goal or end in mind.
In this psalm, the Israelites end by praying to God to destroy
the oppressors. The imagery is explicit and disturbing:

> Happy shall he be who requites you
>   with what you have done to us!
> Happy shall he be who takes your little ones
>   and dashes them against the rock!

The psalmist is seeking more than revenge: this is a request
for the total destruction of the oppressive forces. The
imagery is disturbing, especially in our contemporary
context where we have become sensitised to the abuse of
children. Disturbing as the imagery is, it has something
important to convey to us. Theoretically it suggests that we
cannot have a spirituality of liberation which does not result
in action. Instead, action has to be an integral dimension of
our spirituality. In other words, as well as contemplating,
we must also be commandos for the sake of liberation; we
have to be acting – not just prepared to act. For the Black
Church this means a reorientation.

On the one hand, the Black Church is good at finding
ways of correcting the symptoms of social injustice: for
example, as mentioned above, the Church nurtures good
students in order to counter poor standards in education.
On the other hand, there is an unwillingness to address the
concrete social structures which are the real cause of distress.

In only one denomination has there been a sustained effort to establish Black schools, and very few churches are involved in school support groups. This is what Valentina Alexander means by 'passive resistance'. A reorientation means moving from passive resistance to active resistance; confronting the symptoms and also the structures.[18]

A new vision

There are several points of convergence between *Independent Intravenshan* and Psalm 137. Combined, these two songs provide insight for a new angle on ecclesiology for the Black Church – that is, an ecclesiology which takes seriously the need to affirm and empower all who enter the church doors. This new dimension to our ecclesiology prioritises a spirituality of liberation.

First, we must see the Church as a radical institution offering a countercultural and alternative existence. For Black Churches to become radical institutions means finding new ways of enthusing them with the kind of independence of thought and radical praxis which are at the roots of their formation in Britain. We have now reached a time when Black Churches have to stop living off the radical moves of their founders in the 1950s and 1960s and begin to find a radical spirituality to address the pressing needs of today. To be a countercultural institution means working *against* particular forces within our faith communities. A spirituality of liberation must work to defeat sexist practices and patriarchal structures within the Church. It must seek out ways to teach all within the Church that sexism is a sin. It should seek out processes and practices which affirm the work and life of Black women, so that women are also encouraged to minister and lead churches. However, a spirituality of liberation must also work *with* particular forces within the faith community. For example, ubiquitous single-parenting within Black communities means that the Church has to articulate a spirituality which affirms single parents. It must recognise the need to provide support, instead of treating single parents with suspicion and condemnation. This does not mean that the Church should stop preaching about marriage and family life, but instead, that it must also recognise that there is more than just one form of family unit within the Black community. A spirituality of liberation would affirm the parenting role within our communities.

Second, a spirituality of liberation will constantly seek out new ways of ensuring that the freeing power of Christ is experienced by all. This means continually challenging the ways in which oppressive forces are validated and enshrined within Church structures and Church cultures. This is vitally important if Black Churches are to be a place where people bruised by life can find solace and redemption. To make this prophetic thought a concrete reality, a spirituality of liberation must check the prejudice, which lingers in Black Churches, towards social undesirables. As mentioned above, upwardly mobile Black Churches need to be especially vigilant about class-prejudice and disability oppression within their ranks. Equally important is the area of homosexuality. I have been party to numerous discussions about the Black Church and homosexuality. At best, Black Christians talk about 'hating the sin and loving the sinner'. This kind of evangelical dualism fails to grasp the relationship between humanity and sexuality. Homosexuality is integral to the humanity of gays and lesbians. At worst, Black Christian arguments are irrational, emotional and viciously hostile. None of these options 'ride di staam'.

Finally, a spirituality of liberation must counter the ways in which Black people validate their own oppression. For Black Christians this means critically engaging with liturgy, hymnody, language and other aspects of Church culture to evaluate its effects upon a marginalised faith-community. This also means being concerned with the ways in which our quest for liberation may result in the marginalisation of another group: for example, the establishment of men's groups to build male presence in the Church may simply reaffirm patriarchy. Therefore all quests for liberation must be dialogic, exchanging concerns, ideas and perspectives with church members. A spirituality of liberation cannot result in the liberation of some, at the expense of the rest.

As I said at the beginning of this chapter, worshipping in the Black Church has kept me sane as a Black man in Britain. The love, fellowship and nurture of my local church ensure that I have the opportunity to become an educated servant, rather than an endangered species, in a context of racial subordination. Furthermore, the Church promotes a system of thought and action which ensures the spiritual and psychological well-being of African–Caribbean British people. However, a spirituality of liberation encourages us to go further than the kinds of limited liberative focuses which we have used for so long. Instead we are encouraged to embed deep into our spirit an understanding of the Black Church in which affirmation and empowerment is brought to bear on oppression resulting from gender, class, homosexuality and disability.

2 What kind of freed slaves worship in the slavemaster's Church? Black resistance in White Churches in Britain

It's amazing when I think about it now! As a child, I never thought that White people were truly Christian. I was indoctrinated by the conversations of Black adult Christians to believe that our spirituality was better than the cold, staid and unwelcoming experience of White Christianity. Thankfully later, as a theological student, I realised that this kind of ecclesiastical reasoning was a reflection of ignorance. We had learned our remnant theology from White American denominations which had encouraged us to dismiss other traditions. In the USA dismissing other traditions was influenced by a history of separatism, but in Britain it served other purposes: for example, pastors and elders would dismiss other traditions in order to maintain the loyalty of Black Christians. We were also suspicious because of what the White Christians did to us in the social world.

It was not unusual to hear adult Black Christians talk socially about incidents of racial abuse or racial discrimination perpetrated against them by White people who were members of White Christian denominations. A Christian 'brother' once said to my Dad, 'Me boss say him a Christian, but him nar promote none a di Black people'. This kind of experience reflected the way that 'race' was used as a litmus test for 'being saved'. In other words, we learned to judge White Christians by their estimation and

PART II

Black Christians and representation

3 The Masai have a point: Black male sexual representation and Christology

A Black man in [...]ingham was beaten up by a racist gang. I went on th[...]h to protest the event; yet another attack on a memb[...] he Black community. However, what was interesting [...] his attack was that the assailants had beaten the man [...] his groin and genital area. It was as if they had wan[...] destroy his reproductive capabilities. Also, as the m[...] been out walking with his White girlfriend at the [...] the attack, it was more sinister still. The conversa[...] llow protesters confirmed these suspicions: comment[...] e reasons for the attack, some people were saying, [...] use he had a White girlfriend and they did n[...] a'. Others suggested, 'White people have always be[...] of the Black penis – the gang were simply reverting[...]

After the march I began to [...] e conversations I had overheard. Could it be th[...] k man's sexual potency was a threat to the Whi[...] was it a case of a violent dislike of Black men w[...] He[...] men? Either way, the Black man was severely [...] attr[...] a possible motive for this act of violence was [...] mo[...] view of Black sexuality.

At church the following day, my se[...] tha[...] issue, or issues, of Black sexual pathology [...] 'ho[...] on after Saturday's events. I began to think of the [...] aro[...] ma[...] I had heard on sexuality. I was aware t[...] Bla[...] xelf[...]ck Pentecostal churches such as my own a c[...] l emphasis is placed on matters of sexuality. Brothers and sisters are encouraged to avoid temptation and to engage in respectable courting procedures. Interestingly, at no point have I ever heard a sermon on the issue of Jesus' sexual life. The only reference I could think of was the emphasis that Pentecostalists place upon Jesus being 'without sin'. Although Black Pentecostalists do not list the sins that Jesus avoided, it is often obvious that reference is being made to sexual sin in particular contexts. For example, I once heard a sermon on 'holiness', where the pastor talked about 'sins of the flesh'. At one point the congregation was admonished to stay sexually pure, so that we could truly be like Jesus. The subtle connection made by the pastor between sexual purity and the life of Jesus is the only time I can recall Jesus' sexual life being mentioned.

As I sat in my seat on this particular Sunday, I stared at the icon of the Black Christ above the pulpit. I wondered what Jesus would have said about yesterday's happenings. The sermon was not bubbling, so I began to make connections in my mind between racialised sexual violence against Black people and Christology – who Jesus Christ is for us today. I asked myself, 'Is there any point where Christology can contest the negative racialised images of Black sexuality?'

The answer came a few weeks later when a friend sent me a picture of a Masai Jesus painted by Robert Lentz. The picture showed Jesus' genitalia, visibly protruding from his garment as he knelt in the posture of Christ the teacher. This icon represented Blackness and sexuality in the person of Christ. For me it provided an important breakthrough because in the icon, sexuality was part of Black identity in a positive way – that is, Black sexuality was represented as a part of God's creation and integral to humanity. I continued to struggle with the connection between Black sexuality and Christology, and this chapter is a part of my continuing reasoning on the matter. Here, I want to address the topic of Black sexual representation in popular culture by linking it to this Masai depiction of Jesus. In seeking to bridge these two disparate discourses – that of Black sexual images in popular culture and that of an African icon – I hope to develop a framework for reformulating a Black Christian response to the politics of Black sexual representation.

Representations

In this chapter, I deal first with Black sexual representations because I believe that these are sites of antagonism where the struggle over racial oppression still prevails.[1] Because representations have power, I believe that liberation activity must be played out in this arena. Second, I want to address the question of Jesus' sexual potency because I believe that this speaks to the contemporary Black Church, as well as beyond it, where there is a paucity of discussion on matters of Jesus' sexual awareness and potency. Finally, I want to explore the interpretative significance of Jesus' sexuality for Black people, particularly the socio-political significance of a Black sexual Christology.

My central thesis is that we must engage in the production of images of Jesus which symbolise the quest for Black socio-political sexual wholeness (a concept drawn from the work of Kelly Brown Douglas, who argues that we must seek social and political healing within the Black community). Let me explain this on two levels. On one level, images of Black socio-political sexual wholeness must reflect the diversity and plurality of sexuality in Black communities. We must take into consideration the fact that sexuality is broader than sexual orientation or genital activity, and encompasses our affections, our physiological arousal and our capacity for the erotic and sensuous.[2] On another level, socio-political sexual wholeness confronts the sources of oppression both inside and outside the Black community. We must be conscious of the ways in which race, gender, class and sexual orientation are mobilised to produce negative representations of Black people. Furthermore we must examine the ways in which, within Black communities, sexism and homophobia result in the marginalisation of women, and of gays and lesbians. In short, a socio-political sexual wholeness seeks to answer the question, 'How can images, icons and even language about God in the Black community confront sexist, racist, classist and heterosexist representations of Black bodies in popular culture?' But first, a word about representations.

Representations are ideological constructions. As ideologies, they function as systems of meaning which interpret life. They emerge from social locations, under the influence of historical, political and economic forces. Within the Black diaspora, in contexts which are made conscious by the politics of Black life, the interweaving of representations and social context is highly politicised – that is to say, Black sexual representations *articulate interests*.[3] Challenging representation is a part of our daily struggle because representations are connected to the maintenance of White racism. In his essay, 'Cultural identity and diaspora', Stuart Hall reminds us to recognise the connection between representation and oppression:

> The ways in which Black people . . . were positioned and subjected in the dominant regimes of representation were the effects of a critical expertise of cultural power and normalisation. Not only, in Said's

'orientalist' sense, were we constructed as different and other within the categories of knowledge of the West by those regimes [but] they had the power to make us see and experience *ourselves* as 'Other'.[4]

From this perspective it is possible to expose political issues around the manufacture of Black sexuality in and through different forms of representation.

Historical precedents

We must begin with the past, because representations have histories which provide us with material for a reunification between past (genealogy) and present.[5] Representations of Black sexuality in White popular culture have antecedents in Graeco-Roman culture and the North African conquest of Spain, and were articulated through the discourses of colonialism, empire and imperialism. In each of these contexts, Black people's sexuality was forced into narrow types through a dialectic of objectification for ideological needs.

Robert E. Hood argues that both Greek and Roman cultures constructed mythological traditions representing Black people with powerfully driven and carnal sexual appetites. For example, Greek myths of the sixth century BCE portrayed half-man, half-beast-like creatures with Negroid features who were said to have large sexual appetites and originate in Africa.[6] Hood argues that Black sexuality became a commodity in these cultures, partly due to such types of mythological notions about Black people. If we accept Hood's arguments, the objectification of the Black body and curiosity over its sexual potency go way back in the European psyche. Hence Black people today need to recognise that they are fighting against deeply ingrained traditions which must be defeated by more than the simple, colour-blind attitudes perpetuated both inside and outside Black communities.

The interplay of context and representation appears a millennium or so later when southern Europe was brought face-to-face with Black bodies during the rule of the Moors. In this context, Black people were the dominant political force. But the combination of Christian symbolism with its good/evil, White/Black dualism, and the tendency of conquered people to demonise their oppressors, fostered a fear and suspicion towards Black bodies and Black sexuality. As a result, Black bodies were often represented in medieval art as grotesque, evil and dangerous.[7] However, as Miles shows, during the 400-year period of European expansion and colonisation, the discourse on Black sexual representation was both sustained and, most significantly, reworked.

The emergence of a system of European colonial settlement began a new era of contact and relationship between White and Black people. Robert Miles reminds us that one aspect of the European rationalisation of slavery and colonisation was the White people's self-appointed role as a 'civilising mission' to bring Black *savages* into Christianity and civilisation.[8] Hence, most representations served to show the African as physically, culturally and ethically inferior.[9] Within this context, notions of African sexual potency were reworked: African women were considered to be especially desirous of sexual intercourse, while African men were thought to possess an unusually large penis and to be virile and lustful.[10] For example, Peter Fryer identifies a plethora of writers, commentators and travellers who produced sexually wanton images of African people.[11] Such images of the so-called physical and animalistic characteristics of Black sexuality advanced a fixed image of the African as being below the European on the scale of human progress, but redeemable through the process of civilisation – naturally, under British colonial rule.

A major reworking of the European and North American representations of African people occurred during the growth and hegemony of science in the eighteenth and nineteenth centuries, when so-called scientific methods were used to define racial difference. It was argued by many European scholars that racial difference was fixed, measurable and related to phenotype and biology.[12] One consequence of scientific racism is that, 'savagery became a fixed condition of the African race, the product of a small brain, and civilisation became an attribute of large-brained White people'.[13] Within this context, images of Black sexuality were understood to be fixed. As Homi Bhabha has suggested, an important feature of imperial discourse was, 'Its dependency on the concept of fixity in the ideological construction of Otherness'.[14] As we shall see, this colonial fantasy is repeated in contemporary stereotypes of Black sexuality.

The contemporary context

Today, representations of Black sexuality circulate in cultural forms as ideologies. These ideologies have progressed beyond their traditional location alongside state-sponsored racism and economic exploitation. Representations have become 'entrenched and institutionalised in literature, media, music, educational and vocational organisations, in the popular consciousness and commonsense reasoning'.[15]

'Today, Black men are [still] portrayed as sexually ravenous, magnificently endowed and threats to White women'.[16] For example, in one programme of the TV detective series *Cracker*, a Black man was portrayed as a serial rapist who attacked White women in order to enact revenge on White people.[17] This episode reinforced the myth of the Black male rapist and the notion of a Black male sexual pathology. Similarly, 'Black women are represented as sexually irresponsible and capable of great sexual stamina'.[18] For example, in the British film, *Peter's Friends*, a light-skinned Black woman is portrayed as the sexually vigorous one in a circle of White middle-class friends. These are examples of the way in which both TV and film portray Black sexuality as more promiscuous and immoral than White sexuality, thereby perpetuating the fantasy of Black sexuality and the Black body as an icon of sexual dysfunction.[19]

An exploration and critique of representations of Black sexuality

Many Black female and male intellectuals have deconstructed these representations of Black sexuality. For example, Patricia Hill Collins[20] and Robert Staples[21] have both explored the representations of Black male and female sexuality. Their analysis reveals four significant points. First, it shows that today's images are grounded in the racialised images of the past. Second, they confirm that representations function as controlling ideologies which maintain systems of White power.[22] Third, drawing on the insights of Frantz Fanon, they show that controlling ideologies also reflect the repressed fears of the European civilisation.[23] Fourth, they show that Black people have internalised and reproduced Eurocentric representations: whereas Collins explores this internalisation in the arena of Black female aesthetics, Staples looks at the construction of Black masculinity.

According to Collins, images of Black women grounded in plantation society – such as the 'Mammy' and the 'Matriarch' – both have a correspondence in contemporary diasporan contexts.[24] Also, today's images of Black women as 'domestic workers' and 'domineering castrators' – images which emerge in popular culture – are part of a system of thought that blames Black women for the problem they face, rather than helping to explore the structural forces of inequality which plague Black communities.[25] Collins also explores the multitude of spaces and places used by Black women to counter controlling images, including the development of an alternative epistemology.[26]

According to Staples, in resistance to the denial of certain masculine attributes and as a means of surviving oppression and violent subordination, Black men have adopted certain macho patriarchal values, such as strength and control. Black machismo is big box-office in the 1990s. The movies *Boyz 'n' the Hood, New Jack City, Juice, Fresh* and *Menace II Society* all promote Black masculinist forms. These films reproduce the White stereotype of the aggressive Black male, inadvertently making a racist ideological construction empirically true.[27] Even Mario Van Peebles' *Panther*, the story of the Black Panther Party for Self-Defence (BPP), ignores the intellectual underpinnings of the BPP's practical and down-to-earth radicalism. Instead, Van Peebles focuses on their anti-police aggression, giving only a brief moment of screen-time to the influence on Seale and Newton of the books of Frantz Fanon, Che Guevera and Karl Marx. Staples concludes with a serious warning to Black men: the dominant, White male definitions of manhood make Black machismo a threat to Black women, gays and lesbians – as well as to Black men *ourselves*,[28] because it is a form of 'negative resistance' which fails to challenge racism.

Collins and Staples also show that Black women and men have internalised negative representations of Black sexuality. Collins focuses on issues of skin-colour, hair-texture and general aesthetics,[29] and Staples on such images as the Black 'stud' and the 'supersexed' Black man. Interestingly, the notion of Black male sexual superiority is one myth that very few Black men want to see demythologised. Indeed, Black men often play up to, and reinforce, notions of a superior Black sexual drive and performance. This is clearly demonstrated in the emphasis on Black male sexual prowess, and the size of the Black phallus, in the rap and ragga genres in Black diaspora communities in America, Jamaica and Britain. Furthermore, the dominance of rap and ragga reveals how we, Black straight and gay men, are implicated in the reproduction of 'oversexed' and 'sexually rampant' sexual images.

Opposition from certain Black women and gay Black men has led to a deconstruction of the cultural domination inherent in these representations. For example, bell hooks associates the misogyny of the rap genre with a Black male superimposition of White male sexist, supremacist and patri-archal values.[30] Misogyny in Black music serves to reinforce the economic and social control of Black women, and is therefore an appropriation of a White norm. From another perspective, Black gay men have mobilised in opposition to the development of a narrow, neo-conservative essentialist reading of Black masculinity in Black music and Black film. For example, Black gay cultural critiques have shown how popular culture has codified words like 'faggot', 'punk', 'sissy' and 'queer', in order to control desire, create a space for accusing gays and maintain hetero-patriarchy (the enforced domination of heterosexual male power).[31]

We turn now to the role of Black theology, and particularly Christology, in the battle over representations of Black sexuality.

Jesus' sexuality

The biblical text tells us very little about Jesus' sexuality. As a consequence, much of European Church scholarship has represented him as a celibate – celibacy being a model for a life of devotion.[32] Regarding historical representations of Jesus' sexuality, a very significant breakthrough occurred in Renaissance paintings and sculptures of Jesus, according to Leo Steinberg. Steinberg suggests that numerous representations depict the infant Jesus as naked, in order to reveal that as an infant he was 'complete in all parts'. For Steinberg such paintings suggest that there was an attempt to show Jesus' genitalia in order to reveal what might otherwise be denied: Jesus was sexually aware and had the potential to be sexually active.[33] Unfortunately, this attempt was confined to the artistic world – it did not occur in written form before or after this period. In general, the Church has always deemed eroticism in representations of Jesus as unseemly and out of place. Although Audre Lorde and others have reminded us of the importance of the erotic to a wholesome view of one's humanity,[34] the Church lags way behind. It is thus not surprising that today in the Black Church in Britain, all icons, paintings and sculptures of Jesus cover his genitals, inferring that he was a non-sexual being. This denial is witnessed in discourse on the Black Church in Britain.[35] I want to suggest here a Black Christian re-appropriation of Jesus' sexuality. I begin with an exploration of Christology.

Black Christologies

Black Christologies – that is, how the Jesus of history has been understood as the Christ of faith in Black thought – have given voice to the way in which Black men and women have come to understand how Jesus becomes the mediator of socio-political liberation in the lives of Black people.[36] Black Christology first began to take on a distinctive socio-political significance in the works of James Cone. Cone suggested that Jesus was symbolically (ontologically) Black for Black people today, and was therefore participating in the Black struggle for freedom and liberation.[37] For Cone, Jesus' Blackness meant that he was contemporaneous with Black struggles for freedom from White oppression. The womanist Jacquelyn Grant further developed Cone's hermeneutical manoeuvre. Grant focused upon the humanity of Jesus, as opposed to his maleness, in order to locate the liberative dimension of Jesus in the life-setting of Black women.[38] According to Grant, Jesus as the Christ is an agent of liberation on behalf of the least, including Black women. Hence for Grant, to understand the work of Christ in the world today, that is Black Christology, we must use a multidimensional analysis, focusing on issues of gender as well as race and class oppressions in Black communities.[39]

In recent years, a particularly significant approach to Christology has emerged from Kelly Brown Douglas. Douglas asserts that the liberating work of Christ in the

Black community can be understood as both bifocal and multidimensional. The bifocal aspect takes seriously the oppression manifested both inside and outside Black communities. The multidimensional aspect considers how liberation relates to interlocking systems of race, class, gender and sexuality. In other words, we must take seriously the way in which different forms of oppression interact in order to discover the locus of Christ's liberating work in our communities. Because where Christ is, those who follow Christ must be found, working on behalf of the marginalised.

Finally, another Christology from the liberation tradition is found in this book, where it is suggested that Jesus is Dread for Black people in Britain today. Dread symbolises freedom, power and upliftment. Therefore, the Dread Christ is one who sides with all oppressed people in their struggle against all that denies them full humanity.

If the Black Christ is concerned with holistic Black liberation, then certainly this type of Christology must have something to say to Black men and women who suffer in this world as a direct result of the dysfunctional images of Black sexuality. In other words, because the incarnation informs us that Jesus was fully human, we must also consider how Christ struggles with us against the dehumanisation of Black sexuality. Here, I would like to suggest that the Black Christ, as an image of Black sexual wholeness, is mobilised to support the Black struggle for socio-political sexual wholeness. Let us now explore this idea further.

The Black Christ and sexual representations

Black representations of Christ are a means by which Black theologians can engage in the struggle over Black sexual representations and their implications for Black life. That is, holistic images of Jesus, often considered 'carnal', can point to a socio-political sexual wholeness in which Christ empowers us to confront representations that dehumanise all Black bodies. A socio-political sexual wholeness calls us to struggle collectively against all representations which make the Black body and sexuality issues of shame. The Christ we serve must enable us to confront those who perpetuate demeaning images of Black sexuality. More importantly, a socio-political sexual wholeness must enable us to reformulate Black sexuality so that it becomes the focus of celebration, responsibility and inclusivity. However, such a task should be approached with severe caution, because it is impossible to find one universal, liberative image for a Black socio-political sexual wholeness. Multiple images must therefore be produced to facilitate dialogue between all areas of Black life. If we are only concerned with traditional heterosexual images of Black sexuality, then our liberating thrust will be limited. There are others within the Black community – including Black gays and lesbians – who are also involved in the business of resistance, of over-coming and reconstructing our sexuality in response to the freeing power of the Black Christ.

In the light of the limitation of all icons, I would like to suggest the *Lion of Judah* icon by Robert Lentz (Figure 1) as one image which can be mobilised, in a limited way, as part of this struggle. In my reading, this icon of Jesus is a significant contribution to the struggle for Black socio-political sexual wholeness. Lentz depicts Jesus as a Masai warrior instead of as a European, as is customary. The mixing of Greek and African iconography itself represents the dialectic of cultures and religion in Black diaspora cultures such as my own. The Masai Christ is enthroned in a series of spheres and squares, identifying his unification of time and eternity. In other words, this is a Christ of wholeness. He is surrounded by four winged creatures (the evangelists), each holding a gospel book. The squatting position of the Christ means that his genitalia are visible underneath his robes. In other words, the icon depicts Jesus as a Black warrior and a Black sexual being.

By representing the Black Christ as a warrior, the icon bespeaks Black liberation through Black struggle. It moves beyond the crucified Jesus to the Black Christ the victor, the one who *has* and *will* overcome. For Black diasporan struggle, the image of Christ the warrior is fecund with meaning. While I am aware of the masculinist overtones of this particular warrior imagery, I am also aware of the ability of Black people to identify with the liberating work of Christ without gender inversion of masculine imagery.[40] From this perspective, warrior imagery can resonate with the life-setting of Black children struggling to get an education in under-resourced schools – or even with Black adults fighting for decent housing, employment and education. Likewise such imagery speaks to Black people whose Blackness makes them criminals in a racist criminal justice system; or simply to Black men such as myself who find that we are prejudged as being less than human in almost every multiracial context in which we operate. Most importantly the Black warrior speaks to all Black men and women engaged in the construction of a Black sexual wholeness in the midst of racialised stereotypes which depict Black people as less than human.

Our second concern is representing the Black Christ as a sexual being. By doing so, we make Christ relevant to the

Black struggle for socio-political sexual wholeness. This is because the Black sexual Christ symbolises Christ's involvement in this aspect of our liberation struggle. In other words, giving Jesus genitalia means that we appropriate the sexuality of the Black Christ as a symbol of our liberation, and thereby turn a sign of 'Otherness' into a signifier of identity. By affirming the image of a Black sexual Christ, we acknowledge our identity as full human beings where our sexuality is a full part of our humanity. However, if we take seriously Douglas' concerns over the bifocal and multidimensional implications of a Black Christ, then there are other issues we must consider – namely, that as well as confronting the racist hegemony of Black sexual representations, we also have to confront the role we, as Black people, play in the reproduction of less-than-human representations of Black male and female sexuality. This means that we must be critical of films, music and other media produced in Black communities which represent Black people sexually as less than fully human.

Conclusion

I am not sure how helpful my analysis would be to the Black man who was severely beaten. Neither am I sure of the implications of this kind of iconography for Black churches in Britain, where conservative views towards Black sex and sexuality are normative. However, if the Black Church is ever to take seriously the cross of Jesus, which demands a radical commitment to fighting injustice, then sexuality is one area in which open, honest and democratic debate is necessary. This analysis is partially geared to this end. It is also important to explore issues emerging from this study which do have direct implications for the Black Church – that is, if Jesus' sexuality is taken seriously in our Christology, then we have to think seriously about how Black theology becomes a catalyst for serious thinking about Black humanity and Black sexuality. This analysis can be further explored in the area of Black pastoral care.

In recent years there has been a steady increase in texts which explore counselling by and for Black people. In the USA, pastoral studies have taken seriously the need to question and evaluate attitudes towards Black sexuality. However, in the UK very little, if any, material exists on Black pastoral care and Black sexuality. Hence, I would like to begin the process of developing dialogue in this area by making a few suggestions in light of the observations made above.

First, we must end the silence over negative representations of Black sexuality. Audre Lorde reminds us of the sin of silence in the lives of Black people, and of how we cannot be fully whole until we confront that which causes our oppression.[41] The present conspiracy of silence fails to counter the internalised negative representations of Black sexuality manifested in the self-destructive sexual behaviour in Black diaspora communities. The Church, and those involved in leadership, cannot remain silent on issues of Black sexual representation.

Second, we must see the Black sexual Christ as a way of reconnecting Black sexuality with Black spirituality. One of the characteristics of an internalised Black sexual pathology is the presentation of Black sexuality as dirty and lurid. A Black socio-political sexual wholeness, which comes from seeing Jesus as a sexual being, can reclaim sexuality by ensuring that it is a fundamental aspect of God-given human life. The Masai Jesus informs us that sexuality transcends the sexual act, and is part of our 'lives together in community, as we engage in self-understanding in the knowledge of God.'[42]

Third, we must seek socio-political sexual wholeness. By wholeness, I mean the destruction of the historical and dominant representations of Black sexuality, and also a recognition of the varieties of Black sexual expression within Black communities. Finally, there must also be a celebration of our sexuality as part of our humanity. Only by seeking such wholeness within the Church will we begin to empower Black Christians by giving them the spiritual and intellectual resources needed for engaging in the cultural warfare which is raging daily on every television screen and advertising billboard, and in every cinema presentation.

4 Art and soul: Black Muslim art and Black theology

The *Revelations* series of photographs by Faisal Abduallah and Clive Allen is a creative, philosophical approach to art which uses human subjects in portraiture. By placing Black men and Black women in positions of significance within traditional biblical scenery, the pictures disrupt and overturn images which represent the exclusive dominance of White, Western males. For Faisal and Clive, their work represents a profound link between iconography and politics: images have the power to change perspectives and actions. In this case, the viewer is encouraged to consider the significance of introducing issues of race, gender and Islamic beliefs into biblical imagery. For the Black theologian, these narratives present a 'reservoir of meaning'[1].

Several pieces of work are of considerable interest. First, *The Last Supper I* (Figure 2) depicts the Last Supper with Black men and women dressed in Muslim/African clothing. Interestingly, one of the characters is carrying a gun, the symbolism of which cuts across time and space, and introduces the issue of gun-culture so pertinent in Black diasporan communities. Historically speaking, this image suggests that Black people were and are part of this biblical scene. Furthermore, race and gender presuppositions are challenged by recasting all the characters as Black and some as females. The second picture, *The Last Supper II* (Figure 3) depicts the same characters but dressed in contemporary street-fashion. Here the characters look at the viewers,

drawing them into the scene and requesting their participation in the examination of the subjects at hand. Here the
gun symbolism is used provocatively to communicate power.
The juxtaposition of *The Last Supper I* and *II* suggests a
progression: that the Last Supper is by no means a closure
(the last); instead, it is a continuing event in which we are
all to participate.

In a third picture, *Da Resurrection* (Figure 4), two bare
feet face the viewer directly, with a John Doe name-tag on
the big toe identifying the anonymous person as a 'Negro'.
The image challenges the viewer to contrast the biblical
concept of resurrection with an image of death – in this
case, the resurrection of Christ with the death of a Negro.
By juxtaposing concepts of spiritual life (resurrection) and
racial death (Negro), the artists facilitate a dialogue between
Christian life and Black subordination – an acute matter in
Black theology.

Finally, *The Struggle is Ordained* (Cover), portrays a Black
Christ with his right hand raised to reveal the blood-stains
left by the crucifixion. While this image parodies a similar
depiction in Catholic iconography (once predominant in
West Indian[2] homes), it subverts by substituting a Nubian
in the place of the traditional Catholic Aryan. Furthermore,
by relating the concepts of blood, struggle and race, the
viewer is asked to place Jesus in the role of a Black Messiah.

In conversation with the twenty-six year-old Black
Muslim artist Faisal Abduallah, I wanted to make connections between *Revelations* and Faisal's life-story – because his
art is closely connected to his experience of Christianity
and Islam. Furthermore, one of my central interests as a
Black theologian is the way in which *Revelations* mediates
pertinent issues between and on behalf of Black Muslims
and Black Christians in Britain today.

A conversation with Faisal Abduallah

RB   How did you get into art?

FA   From a very early age, I enjoyed painting and drawing.
     By ten or eleven, I'd decided that I wanted to go to
     art school. My parents were dead against it; they
     wanted me to go to medical school and be a paediatri-
     cian. I reacted against that, and continued to take art
     in the sixth form at school. I had a very good teacher
     who guided me through it, and said I could go on
     and do a degree. I thought, 'Me, do a degree?' I left
     college and went to Harrow, and then to Central St
     Michael's School of Art, to do my degree and from
     there straight to do my Masters at the Royal College.
     Things have sort of developed from there. While I
     was at Central St Michael's, I went to America to
     study in Boston.

RB   Boston has a reputation as a racist city.

FA   Yeah, but studying there was a complete revelation
     that changed my life. Before going to America I had
     no space to accommodate Black history and Black
     politics. My work was very abstract in line, form and
     colour, and in the technical aspects of my practice.
     But going to America led me to feel quite ashamed.
     I would talk to White Americans who told me about
     Black history, and made me aware that there was a lot
     to it. Then I began to go to the library and read up
     about Black intellectuals such as Frantz Fanon and W.
     E. B. Du Bois, and artists like Norman Lewis, Lang-
     ston Hughes and other Black painters. Now I'd been
     studying art for three or four years in institutions in
     England and I'd never heard of these guys. Everything

just did a 360-degree turn when I learned about the Harlem Renaissance – the whole culture of dance, music, art and poetry. While I was there I was painting a lot of quite abstract pictures. I continued to work in that style, but the content of the work began to change: I had a reason for making the work, there was a lesson that I had to teach to the viewers; I thought I had a responsibility from that point on. And when I came back from America, I immediately began to do work based around Malcolm X, making a comparison between him and the rappers Ice Cube and A Tribe called Quest who were just coming up in the late 1980s and early 1990s. I made an installation for my degree show whereby you'd walk into a space with screen-prints suspended from the ceiling. The viewer would walk into a tunnel with an image of Malcolm X on either side. As they went to the back of the space, there was a speaker playing rap-tracks mixed with speeches by Malcolm X. As you walked out of the space, on the back of the prints of Malcolm X were the images of rappers. So as you walked into the void you saw Malcolm Xs and as you came out there were new Malcolm Xs – suggesting that his message is still carrying on in different forms, even though he [Malcolm] is no longer here. I thought that these rappers were new icons for the 1990s. It was quite prophetic.

RB If going to the USA introduced Black politics into your work, what caused the introduction of religion, and in particular the biblical images found in the *Revelations* exhibition?

FA My interest in religion also started when I was in America, and I began to read the autobiography of

Malcolm X. I was staying in Roxbury, where he was
brought up, and I became intrigued with his life and
began to see similarities between it and my own life.
I was reading stuff in the book and thought,
'Blimey!' I wasn't going to read it in the first place: I
only came across it because I went to a Puerto Rican
wedding with a friend. He kicked the book from
beneath his bed while he was changing, and said, 'Do
you want to read it?' And I said, 'I don't want to read
that rubbish!' – but he insisted. I read it while I was in
the USA, and carried on reading it when I got back to
England. But also, while I was in the USA, I used
to listen to the radio. On one station, there was this
guy speaking quite articulately about how African—
Americans spend more on drugs than on food per year.
I kept listening to the programmes, and thought that
this guy was really empowering. I asked one of the
brothers in the same building as me, who the guy on
the radio was, and he said, 'It's Farrakhan'. One of the
guys at college was a Muslim, so I asked him to take me
to a mosque. So one Sunday, two Nation of Islam guys
came, big six-foot guys, in a big Cadillac, extremely
smartly dressed, and drove me to the mosque. And I
think that was it – I felt at home then. They gave me
knowledge of my history – why I had not advanced for
400 years; why I got taken to this Western hemisphere;
the powers that be which were working against me and
trying to some extent to terminate my existence. This
information not only uplifted me spiritually, but it also
gave me a political standpoint, a voice, and it gave me
back my history and myself. From that point on I
became very conscious about spirituality in my work.
Revelations, which happened five years later, was a result
of that experience.

RB   It's interesting that you should mention the autobiography of Malcolm X because for me, reading Malcolm was a real turning-point. I read it when I was at secondary school, almost by accident, because my history teacher said, 'You can do your history project on Martin Luther King or Malcolm X'. I chose Malcolm X because I didn't know anything about him. But it ended up being a real turning-point. I began to ask questions about Black Christianity, and to look for politics and a Black nationalist identity within it. In contrast, despite your Black Pentecostal upbringing, Malcolm X led you to the Nation of Islam. Why was that?

FA   Malcolm X's book kept putting over the point that Christianity had made us complacent, non-violent and willing to accept what we had been given, making the excuse that we would get our reward in heaven. The creative notion which the book gave me was the concept of 'milk and honey'. I thought to myself, if I can go to the shop and buy milk and honey, then I want my social and political 'milk and honey' here and now as well. Also, he said that we could take certain actions in terms of liberating ourselves and making ourselves heard. For me, Islam had all the desired effects. Islam was a starting-point for investigating things.

RB   What helped me look to Christianity was making the distinction between the religion of the slavemaster and the religion of the slave. Many slaves bought into the slavemaster's religion – that Christianity was something to make you passive, humble and not conscious. But there was slave Christianity that was much more concerned with resistance and rebellion. So in Jamaica in the last century there were national heroes such as Sam

Sharpe, Paul Bogel and William George Gordon – all of whom were Christians who led rebellions against their slavemasters and oppressors. I guess I found answers to some of the questions raised by Malcolm within Black Christian history. I know that your parents are church-goers, your Dad's a pastor and that you spent a lot of time in church, so why didn't the Church provide any answers for you?

FA   For me, going to church as a child simply meant learning Bible stories. It wasn't empowering or a platform for political empowerment – it wasn't into any of those things. So only when I went away to the USA, and came back, did I realise that there was more to Christianity than teaching me about a blonde-haired, blue-eyed Christ. My Bible had such images on each page: there were pictures of Moses as White, with a long blond beard and blue eyes. But when you break it down, this guy is from Africa! We even had pictures of a European Jesus on the walls in the front room and in the hallway of the house.

RB   We used to have those as well, including the ones with the eyes that followed you around the room.

FA   Me and my Dad use to have long debates about it. There is a funny story about this, because my Dad turned Christian before I was born, because he'd met Jesus just like I'm talking to you now. So I asked him, 'Dad, tell me what colour Jesus was when you met him?' He said, 'Why do you want to know that? He came to save the world, so why does it matter what colour he is?' So I asked him whether Jesus in his vision was like the man in the pictures in the front room and the hallway. It took him about half-an-hour with me going at him, before he said that the Jesus he'd seen wasn't a White man. So I said, 'What colour was he then?' – and he said, 'He was a Black man'. For me that was like a complete revelation, because my father never spoke about race. He was a pastor and always saw himself as neutral. So I was blown away by his reply.

RB   So it was almost as if there was a consciousness of Black presence within the Bible – that the Bible had been inspired by African forces, but with no explicit acknowledgement of the fact?

FA   That's what visual representation does – and that's what I seek to address: the notion that visual images have the power to shift people's vision of the world. There are a large number of people who can't read, but they can *read* a visual image. Visual images are a profound and powerful way to try and shift views of the world.

RB   Actually, one of the chapters in this book, 'The Masai have a point', asks whether visual images can change the way in which Black Christians understand themselves. But I'm trying to explore both Blackness and sexuality as areas in which the Black Church needs to shift its thinking. Returning to the *Revelations* series, some most of the powerful images were *The Last Supper* pictures (Figures 2 and 3). What was the thinking behind those two images?

FA   I had the idea for *The Last Supper* about two years before it came to fruition. I was disturbed by the number of artists from the Renaissance period – the likes of Leonardo da Vinci and Michelangelo – and even contemporary painters like Stanley Spencer, depicting what they thought the Last Supper was like. Their paintings are artistic interpretations of the story, and there is a certain artistic licence – but in too many Last Suppers there is a similar ethos. My aim was to create a powerful image which would empower young Black people in London, and place them within that historical context and give them something to make them feel that they were history – not *part* of history but that they *were* history. The main focus of the work was the concept of a Black Messiah. I used twelve people (as opposed to thirteen): six men and six women.

RB   Explain the use of the women in these pictures. I mention this is because both Black and White students have responded positively to these images. However, one criticism from Black women is that the Jesus-figure in the middle is looking at the men – so even though women are there, they are on the margin behind the men. It's almost as if you were dealing with a proto-womanism in these pieces.

FA   Regarding the first point, the women are there because women are a part of history. In terms of biblical history they have been marginalised – represented only as bodies for domestic reasons or for times of sorrow. They are not represented as playing an active role in biblical history. Yet they did! They were there in the context and in the words. So I was trying to bring them back into the picture through visual imagery. Regarding the second point, I can illustrate my thoughts by mentioning a debate I had recently about the gender positioning in this icon. The person I was talking to commented that the photograph had been constructed in such a way as to get the viewer to focus immediately on the Christ-figure in the middle. I replied that this was because the viewer is always led to believe that the male is the dominant sex, so is immediately attracted to the male figure in the middle. This focusing is simply a construction, because the figure in the middle is *not* necessarily Christ. Christ could be the one carrying the nine-millimetre hand-gun. This picture is a mirror: it shows where you are coming from and what is important to you.

RB   I thought that the character in the middle was Jesus, making the sign of the peace, and the person carrying the gun was Judas.

FA   That is one way of looking at it. But when this work is on display, a chair sits in front of this piece of work for the thirteenth person. There are twelve people in the picture. So who is the thirteenth person? Some say it's the camera, but the thirteenth person could be Jesus, Judas or even another disciple. So the piece is open-ended. And I haven't said who the thirteenth person is. I've shown the picture in many places, and only a former tutor noticed that there were just twelve people in the picture. For me, this image is all about Black African iconography. Its very important to place my people in positions of power, so that they can use these images to replace the ones on their walls.

RB   Why the intermixing of Islamic and Christian imagery? You have some men in Islamic skull-caps, and some of the women wearing veils, within a setting that is associated with Christianity. It's like the 1950s in America when, for a few years, Muslims and Christians were much closer than now.

FA   I think it's important to put aside our difference. Islam has a lot to contribute to the present situation, as does Christianity. So when I construct a picture, I like it to contain as many different images as possible. For me, space, time and light are the three elements which are a part of my work. The time element is the most important. You can walk through different levels of time: the pistol is a image of the 1990s, and also a symbol of destruction of Black African people. But you can also see a wooden floor, a curtain, a fifteenth-century table and attire which represents different historical periods and different geography. So it's a walk through time. I have tried to eliminate religious bias so that a Christian, a Muslim or a Jew can all identify with it. Don't get me wrong – it's not a picture to please all; it is my attempt to depict an event which took place.

RB   What about the second picture, *The Last Supper II*? Why did you give the central character, possibly Christ, an Uzi automatic?

FA   Basically, in *The Last Supper I*, I wanted to create a theatrical event which showed people in unity. They are wearing Muslim garments, and they are all real people whom I knew well – so I created a visual unity between them. Now, *The Last Supper II* was a contemporary Last Supper; 'Last Supper' does not really mean it's the last one – it means the beginning. The idea of continuation can be seen in the fact that there is no bread on the table, no food. Bread is a form of nourishment, but the bread I am introducing here is metaphorical, representing knowledge. Hence, while there is no physical bread, there is intellectual bread – the images. The characters are dressed in their own clothes, not only out of respect for who and what they are as individuals, but also to acknowledge that mentally they are united. Because I believe that we can only be physically united when we are mentally united.

All the people in the second picture are united: they have similar goals, principles and read the same Scriptures. But at the same time they are willing to achieve what they want by any means necessary.

RB   What about the Uzi?

FA   The gun can symbolise power – more than one person has a gun. It is important to place Black people in positions of power. Now, I am not saying that they are gun-toting people: these are just images which people can use or interpret as they wish. I instructed everyone in the picture to stare at the camera, because I believe the eyes are a doorway to the soul. I was trying to get the viewers to feel that they were outside *The Last Supper I* but inside the event of *The Last Supper II*. *The Last Supper II* is an event that they could just step into.

RB   Another image in the *Revelations* series is *Da Resurrection* (Figure 4). What's your thinking behind that?

FA   That's one of my favourite pieces.

RB   When I showed it to theology students, they were not sure whether the concept represented an end or a beginning. In the end they settled for both: for some, the two feet with the John Doe name-tag suggests that the Negro is dead and that out of this death something more powerful shall rise. For others, it is a symbol of a living death that many Black people experience.

FA   That's very good. Those are the two best interpretations that I've heard. When the picture was on exhibition, I placed the Bible on one side and the Koran on the other, each held together with cable so that neither could be opened. The whole notion behind this was that individuals can resurrect themselves through Christianity or through Islam. The John Doe tag is what most people get when they leave this realm. It normally has their name and date of birth on it. But the label 'Negro' doesn't indicate that they were part of this society; it makes them anonymous, so to speak. *Da Resurrection*, in its simplest form, talks about the notion of how we can resurrect ourselves through these different sources or channels. But we can also look into ourselves, ignoring Christianity, Islam or Judaism, and still resurrect ourselves. The picture is a mirror. When you look at the picture, you see yourself and ask whether you can resurrect yourself of your own accord and through your own belief-system. I needed to be guided because I was way-off. I needed Islam to guide me; my father needed Christianity to guide him. I know people who have never needed any of those belief-systems but have used their own inner knowledge and intellect to resurrect themselves. But the notion of the Negro as a symbol of Black death and Black life is a valid interpretation. These pieces are icons for people to identify with, and to which they can relate.

RB The exhibition also included several images of a Black Christ, entitled, *The Struggle is Ordained* [front cover image]. I notice now that these are a picture of you.

FA No! The person in the picture is a friend of mine. A lot of people think that it's me because we look alike.

RB OK, that changes my question – I had thought that you'd positioned yourself in the place of Christ. Anyway, there has been a tradition in Britain, primarily through Rastafari, of representing Jesus as Black. But, in the UK context, this is the first Black Christ I have seen without dreadlocks. So what made you call it *The Struggle is Ordained*?

FA   It was a title given by Clive Allen, the guy I worked with on this project. Behind it were my ideas and feelings about the notion that the Saviour of humankind is portrayed as White. As a child, I believed that White people were superior to me simply because the Saviour who had come to teach me about life and the hereafter was White like them. That had a profound effect on me, and on how I dealt with my own people – I was less compassionate towards Black people than White people. By portraying Christ as Black, I began to deal with my own people more compassionately. It was only when I managed to step out of myself, to empower myself through Islam, that I began to understand why I had treated White and Black people differently. I had been bombarded with these White images from an early age, and so I decided to smash the White image and depict Jesus how he was. What I show is not just a representation – it is a fact. The background of the tribe of Judah indicates that Jesus's tribe looked more like me. One of the reasons I created *Revelations* was to show our people's position: we had a seminar on the Black Christ, and I couldn't believe that there were people who thought we didn't need a Black Christ. I thought, 'These people have got to wake up'. Even though Christ's colour didn't matter to them, it mattered to the artist and it matters to the vicar who puts up the image in church.

RB   We have a picture of a Black Madonna and Child in my home church in Handsworth. It was interesting that when it was put up, most of the people who objected to it were Black!

FA   In fact, I have recently re-shot the Black Madonna and
      Child for a programme, *The Art of Identity*, for BBC 2.
      They asked me to respond to a fifteenth-century
      painting by Bellini, *The Madonna in the Meadow*. This
      shows the Madonna and Child in a fifteenth-century
      Venetian landscape – nothing to do with biblical
      history. So what I did was use an urban landscape –
      Harlesden in London. I then dressed the model and
      child in religious clothes and photographed them
      against the backdrop of Harlesden.

RB   I have appreciated the politics behind your pictures,
      and from what you have said, it appears that you are on
      a journey. How do you see your art developing?

FA   I'm currently working on a piece that walks through
      Black English history – it will cover everything. It's an
      extensive look at Black people in London. I think that
      every Black African—Caribbean person has a duty to
      their audience. I am not saying that they should spout
      Black nationalism, telling Black people that all White
      men are devils. We are beyond that kind of thinking.
      Instead, I want a more complex and intellectual
      approach to art which offers people a choice as to
      where they want to go. It's about creating works of art
      that embody Nubian spirituality.

RB   How do you define Nubian spirituality?

FA   For me, Nubian spirituality is something internal,
      about the soul. It's about spiritual awareness – 'the third
      eye'[3] – and is not something I express in words, but
      in my day-to-day living. So my approach to Nubian
      spirituality is about walking a certain path in response

to the history of my African ancestors. My summary of Nubian spirituality is my work.

RB   Many artists and cultural critics in Britain have been reluctant to engage with the spiritual. Instead, they just want to deal with the concrete, and exclude the significance of any reality outside this, and its role in the lives of Black people. It's as if there were no appreciation of the metaphysical.

FA   Yeah, the metaphysical is a very important space. It's a very creative space, which has no limitations and cannot always be put into a context. The metaphysical has the power to transform and empower a nation to overturn what we have previously known.

Closing thoughts

In conclusion, Faisal Abduallah's work represents a starting-point for a reinvestigation of Black Christian iconography in Britain. His work puts the spirituality of art back on the agenda for Black British church communities. Faisal's Islamic/Afrocentric focus provides a much-needed critical machete, cutting down and reshaping so as to mobilise Black people. Furthermore, his commitment to politicising Christian iconography encourages every Black Church to question the social and political export of Black Church iconography.

However, there are still some major issues which require further development. First, although Faisal must be praised for including women in his work, their positioning, posture and colour symbolism in *The Last Supper I* bespeaks mar-

ginality. Womanist theologians in Britain have long argued
for a careful analysis of race and gender politics in order
to challenge the 'either/or' attitude in Black communities.
Womanists posit as an alternative a 'both/and' scenario, in
which gender marginalisation is on an equal footing with
racial subjugation.[4] Second, it is clear that gun-culture in
Black diasporan communities has a varied history. While
the gun has been used as a symbol of Black political
mobilisation (for example, by the Black Panther Party for
Self-Defence), today gun-culture in Black British communities is associated with death, drugs and destruction. Hence,
we must ask, about Faisal's use of the gun-image, what kind
of power is being expressed and on whose behalf? But these
concerns must be placed alongside the fact that, as Faisal
says so eloquently, the artist is on a journey and these images
represent one stage. I look forward to continued critical
dialogue and interaction at his forthcoming exhibitions.

5   Watching you watching me: Black Christians in popular culture

How are the Black Church and Black Christians represented in popular culture? And what political issues emerge from the places and spaces in which we are positioned? There are very few areas of cultural discourse where the Black Church and Black Christianity are mentioned, and even fewer where we are critically explored. Even so, the places where we are seen tells much about critical issues of representation confronting Black Christians in Britain today. I decided that a useful way of identifying these issues would be to keep a diary of significant events during the year, in which I commented on the central themes. Reproduced below are four entries, made between July 1996 and April 1997, and chosen because they cover a range of issues and concerns which emerged throughout the year.

July 1996: Appropriation and exploitation of Black British gospel music

I've just watched *Songs of Praise*. The whole programme was dedicated to the music of Graham Kendrick. It made me think of the appropriation and exploitation of the Black Church tradition by musicians, singers and composers. This kind of thing has a long history in Britain: one only needs to explore the history of rock and roll to witness the appropriation and exploitation of Black musical traditions by White European and American artists. However, some White groups have made a conscious effort to acknowledge the influence of Black music. For example, Eric Clapton, when interviewed for a BBC radio programme, *Desert Island Discs*, talked of his delight in, indebtedness to, and infatuation with, Black rhythm. Indeed, Clapton once recorded Bob Marley's *I Shot the Sheriff* and achieved a Number 1 hit in the USA. A similar confession is made by East 17, a White hip-hop group from East London, who publicly acknowledge their appreciation of Black bands such as Jodici.[1] We might call the efforts of Clapton and others 'the appropriation tradition': here, artists make a conscious effort to acknowledge their sources and give credit where it is due. Such public acknowledgement has a big impact on Black British communities, primarily because the unparalleled African–Caribbean contribution to post-war British popular culture is barely recognised, despite the wholesale adoption of Black expressive cultures in Britain. Indeed, cultural theorists suggest that it is impossible to talk about popular culture in Britain without many references to the influence of Black expressive culture. This does not mean that Black folk are not prone to appropriation: as mentioned below, the Black Church is prone to borrowing from Christian and secular sources.[2]

However, many groups are not so quick to acknowledge Blackness – a classic example of this silent type being the 1970s and 1980s pop band, The Police. Headed by Sting, The Police initially based their success on appropriated reggae music, producing a distinctive White English reggae genre ('*regeatta de blanc*') – remember *Roxanne* and *Message in a Bottle*? The Police's White reggae was a home-grown response to Jamaican reggae, one of the prime musical influences on disaffected White youths in the late 1970s in England. We may call this 'the exploitation tradition', because The Police, although indebted to reggae, made very little effort to acknowledge its influence upon their music. By their silence, the creative expression of Black people is made invisible, and relegated to the background of artistic achievement. This is a form of cultural avoidance which wipes out a people from history – rather like a family which doesn't want to acknowledge that it has Black blood in its veins. This does not mean that Black folk are not also exploitative: there are numerous examples of Black musicians borrowing and stealing from other traditions without giving credit where credit is due.

Issues of appropriation and exploitation emerge in the songs of Britain's leading White gospel songwriter, Graham Kendrick. First, it is clear that Kendrick makes use of Black gospel music – one only has to listen to his album, *Rumours of Angels*, to find the distinctive rhythms and styles of the Black Church. This issue is sharpened by the fact that Kendrick's producer and assistant is Steve Thompson, the son of a Birmingham Pentecostal preacher, born and bred in the Black British Church tradition. Second, despite the appropriation, there is something deeply troubling about Kendrick's use of Black music and Black musicians. This brings me to the issue of exploitation.

Unquestionably, many White gospel artists make use of Black music, but in the traditions of exploitation there is very often little recognition of Black sources or influences. It's amazing that, in a world dominated by copyright issues, in which every artist who 'samples' music has to acknowledge his or her sources, there is among gospel singers an unwillingness to give credit to the influence of Black gospel on White artists. And why should they? I keep forgetting that most White Evangelical Christians still believe in a

colour-blind God – a God who does not see colour. Therefore good Christians don't talk in terms of Black or White,
just good, bad and Spirit-filled. One of the consequences
of denying colour, race and identity is that the racism of
many White evangelicals goes unchecked. By spiritualising
identity, many White songwriters and musicians ignore the
very real issues of racial injustice and social inequality which
affect the lives of Black people in Britain.

In recent years the Black Church has become increasingly
vocal on issues of exploitation. Take, for example, the song
Blues People by Sounds of Blackness, which tells of generations of Black musical exploitation in the USA – in
particular, the decontextualisation of Black music whereby
it is divorced from experience. The track is introduced by
a significant quotation from Langston Hughes:

You've taken my Blues and you've gone
You mix them up on Broadway and fix them up in operas
so that they don't sound like me.
Yep you done taken my Blues and gone
But some day someone is going to stand up for me
and sing about me, Black and beautiful.

Maybe it's time for Black British Christian musicians, songwriters and artists to ask questions about exploitation: in
short, to ask the question, 'Who has taken our blues and
gone?'

November 1996: Misrepresenting Black Church life

I've just finished watching the first three episodes of *Brothers and Sisters*. It reminds me of old-fashioned White anthropologists who would travel to 'deepest, darkest Africa', find and study a remote tribe, and eventually publish a book or paper on the people they'd studied. Usually, the publication described the African tribe as uncivilised, uneducated, primitive, barbaric and crude – but happy. Happily such approaches to anthropology are now generally regarded as racist, parochial and a total misrepresentation of African cultures and world-views. However, a new form of racialised misrepresentation of Black life has raised its head on Friday nights, in the form of *Brothers and Sisters*, a 'soap' set in a Black Pentecostal church, 'somewhere in the North of England'. Like the misinformed anthropologists, the BBC crew responsible for the programme (many of them Black British writers and TV people) have misrepresented Black religious life.

Before I go any further, it's important to acknowledge what many people believe to be structural racism within the BBC. *Brothers and Sisters* is part of a TV package for Black people called *The A Force* which goes on air at around 11.15 p.m. The timing of the broadcast seems to imply that Black viewers are marginal creatures who only appreciate programmes late at night – also, the BBC are reminding Black people that, despite paying their license fees, they are not an important constituency warranting prime-time programming.

Furthermore, *The A Force* is primarily comedy, barring *The Beginner's Guide* series, which injects a few minutes of lightweight Afrocentric history and culture. So in terms of structure, Black comedy gets more time than informed, intelligent Black thinking – an imbalance which has a long history. Back in the days of slavery, plantation owners would cultivate slaves who were gifted at entertaining the White folks. These entertainers were the diametric opposite of the revolutionaries and wise Black people on the plantation, of whom the master was deeply fearful. Interestingly, some slave entertainers managed to use their humour as a vehicle for revolutionary thinking – we shall return to this dangerous idea later.

Back to *Brothers and Sisters*. There is a lot of positive material in the programme: the focus on life in a Black Pentecostal church, the attempt to explore often-ignored issues – for example, by offering a positive image of Black homosexuals, or by including the all-too-common discovery of the existence of children from first relationships or marriages in the Caribbean by the families of their remarried parents in England. Also, there is a real attempt to provide well-rounded and multidimensional Black characters. Take, for example, the oldest son of the Peters family, Jonathon: He represents a tough-minded but tenderhearted Black man, who is aware of his family responsibilities and also sensitive to his own needs and aspirations as a Black gay man. However, there is much within the programme that is downright negative – such as racist stereotypes which caricature and misrepresent Black people.

I have two main objections to the series. First, the writers must have studied some remote and unrepresentative Black church on which they based their central ideas about Black church life. For example, the language is all wrong: Black churches have their own language systems, and have a brilliant way of incorporating Scripture, proverb and allegory as part of their dialogue about God, life and the world. Here, the writers simply represent the Black church members as mimicking White British culture, with a few added 'Amens' and 'Hallelujahs'. The message is that Black churches are Black people trying to be like White people, with a few extra Amens. This may have something to do with the fact that it was written by Black people whose understanding of African–Caribbean church life is limited.

Second, the soap genre used by the writers leads to another misrepresentation. Because it's soap, everyone has to have a skeleton in the closet. We need look no further than the leading Peters family for examples: the older son comes out as gay, the daughter has had an abortion, and the stalwart deceased father (a pastor) has an illegitimate child in Jamaica. Not only is this sequence of events unrealistic, but also it is explored and resolved in a way which lacks sensitivity and awareness of Black Pentecostals. Black people were promised something new within the genre – but we have received nothing. We may as well be watching *EastEnders*, *Brookside* or *Neighbours* set in a Black church, rather than a soap that examines and explores Black Pentecostalists in Britain.

In short, *Brothers and Sisters* is not a realistic presentation of Black church life – it is simply an imaginary drama set in the Black church. What a shame the writers did not talk to people who could have highlighted areas of real dramatic potential, thereby preventing many of the flights of fancy being passed off as real representation! In Black history there are traditions of using comedy to effect social change – for example, the Anansy stories from the Caribbean, and the Br'er Rabbit stories from the USA, both use the comic to challenge perceptions radically. Black people can thus draw on a comic tradition which could contain alternative ingredients for a Black soap. Maybe, by the end of the series, the programme will have (for me) redeemed itself, by saying something significant, meaningful and challenging about Black Pentecostalists in Britain.

February 1997: Negotiating the old grey areas

I've just got round to buying the new album by Nu Colours (which is also called *Nu Colours*). Without doubt the *Nu Colours* album displays the vocal talent, musical creativity and aesthetic sensibilities traditionally associated with Black gospel music in Britain. Vocal talent is expressed in low tempo, soul-stirring tracks, such as, *Yes I Will*, and the more up-tempo dance track, *Special Kind of Lover*. Their musical creativity blends together gospel/soul themes and rhythms to produce a new inspirational tradition following in the footsteps of Paradise, the London Community Gospel Choir and Brian Powell. Aesthetic sensibility is demonstrated in the soulful, rhythmic moods, feelings and 'grooves' – take, for example, the soulful crooning of *You Took Me to Heaven*, and the melodic, easy tempo of *The Heart's a Messenger*. However, despite the undeniable talent of the London-based quartet, the *Nu Colours* album displays all the old grey areas of Black gospel crossover. Crossing over (between gospel and mainstream pop music) without going under is a delicate art involving keeping one's musical feet in two camps. The first camp is the gospel music scene; the second is the secular music industry. The first camp is primarily concerned with lyrical integrity, biblical identification and existential wrestling. The second camp is concerned with economic viability, commercial content and cosmetic aesthetics. We begin with the interests of the first camp.

Black gospel tradition

Lyrical integrity concerns commitment to the Gospel of Jesus. After all, it is the living Word and living-out the

Word, which provide the raw material for Black gospel music in the UK tradition. In practice, lyrical commitment means being explicit about one's faith and commitment to Jesus in the words of your songs. If the music doesn't mention God, Jesus or salvation, then it is being watered down.

Black gospel music is also concerned with biblical identification – that is, the use of biblical terms, themes, narratives and expressions in the lyrics. Part of the strength of Black choir music is its biblical identification. Some of the classic spirituals in the African–American tradition demonstrate the power of retelling the biblical story. Contemporary gospel artists have maintained this tradition, and on occasion made hermeneutical connections with contemporary socio-political issues. For example, a part of the chart success of The Winan's *Let My People Go* in the mid 1980s was its strong sense of biblical identification and contemporary social resonance: the association of Israel's bondage in Egypt with the Black oppression in South Africa. Biblical identification is related to lyrical integrity in the sense that both place a premium on the Bible as a central resource.

The final concern of the first camp is existential wrestling. Deep, soul-searching, existential wrestling is a central concern of Black gospel music. Whether addressing the question of theodicy, exploring a personal failing or praying for a friend or enemy, the songs delve deep into human experience and try to make sense of tragedy – another main focus. At gospel concerts the songs which delve into human experience are often greeted with the greatest audience response and the most participation. One reason for their appeal is their ability to make sense of tragic despair and give hope in the midst of calamity. Classics like Vanessa Bell Armstrong's *Oasis* represent the best of existential wrestling. Hence, an audience 'has church' (i.e. has a worship experience) when songs touch the soul, open the heart and soothe the mind. To avoid mining the existential seams of Black Christian existence is another way of failing to do justice to the music. Gospel music which fails to wrestle with the absurd or the tragic, in the words of one Black Christian, 'Ain't saying nuffing'.

The secular music industry

The second camp is the music industry, which is concerned with economic viability, commercial content and cosmetic aesthetics. Economic viability concerns sell-ability: music which doesn't sell won't be promoted. So, in order to make money, Black gospel music has to appeal to the interests and tastes of secular Black and White markets. Living in a secular nation, with a declining public spirituality, is profoundly challenging to the dogmatic lyrical integrity required by the gospel-music tradition. In short, gospel bands have to revise their music significantly in order to make it appeal to the secular market.

This brings us to the second concern: commercial content. Commercial content is concerned with the genre – specifically with the lyrics and music. The secular music industry demands lyrics that sell in the market-place – so gospel bands have to sing about what the market wants to hear or will be interested in. For example, every song on the *Nu Colours* album might be considered a form of love-song – but whose love? Because the genre requires ambiguity, it's impossible to sing explicitly about biblical images, metaphors or narratives. Likewise, the music has to relate to current trends, 'groove' and musical sensibilities. Regarding lyrics, most gospel artists compromise by adopting the inspirational music genre, whereby they use terms, images and concepts which are resonant in each camp. For example, Nu Colours use the words *Special Kind of Lover* and *Joy* as titles of songs: in the gospel camp, the first title conjures images of the love of God; in the music industry camp it signifies love between two human partners. Similarly the song *Joy* communicates a specific gift of the Spirit in the gospel camp, while in the music industry camp it refers to an ecstatic feeling. Regarding a musical compromise, there is less tension. This is primarily because contemporary gospel, over the past three decades, has moved closer to contemporary Black music. Moreover, as many gospel artists, particularly in the USA, move between gospel and secular music with impunity, it has become very difficult to define what is and what is not authentically a gospel-music form.

Finally, the secular music industry camp is concerned with cosmetic aesthetics – that is, the 'image' of the band, as well as the emotional weight and content of the music. For gospel bands already constrained by the restraints of commercialism, cosmetic aesthetics further limit the depths of existence and experience which they can explore. In short, gospel bands compromise by engaging in varying degrees of lightweight existential contemplation. This means that they only moderately engage with serious spiritual matters, which are often submerged beneath a bombardment of heavy-duty rhythm and music, or drum and bass. An example of moderate engagement can be found on the Nu Colours album in the song *Yes I Will*, where the band sings of unconditional support. An example of submerged lyrics can be found in the London Community Gospel Choir (LCGC) chart hit, *Fill My Cup*, from the late 1980s. LCGC's hit was a parody of a church song often sung as a chorus. They actually sang about the in-filling of the Spirit and sanctification (cleansing). However, the lyrics were sub-merged beneath a techno-disco beat that cut and mixed the lyrics so that 'Fill my cup' was only the discernible line.

Nu Colours play the crossover game well. Songs like *Special Kind of Lover, Desire, Yes I Will, Joy, You Took Me to Heaven, You Give Me More, Don't Mind Waiting, The Heart's a Messenger* and *I Pray* sit neatly in the ambiguous world of crossover gospel. However, *Back Together Again, Did You Wanna Go Back (To When), Tomorrow Love* and *Thinking About You*, are closer to secular rhythm and blues love-songs. Even so, I would contend that any of this last group of songs, sung in the spiritually charged mood of a gospel concert, could well be treated as contemporary gospel – especially if one of the band were to give a spiritual interpretation before singing the song, so that the lyrics were made to resonate with concepts and ideas associated with the love of God. Such polysemy bears testimony to the skill and craft of crossover music. Despite displaying all the old grey areas of crossover, Nu Colours represent a new generation who have attempted to gain competence in this genre. How long they survive will depend on their ability to negotiate the two camps.

April 1997: The directory of diocesan domination

Every year, I receive a diocesan handbook from the Anglican Diocese of Birmingham. It keeps me up to date with new names and addresses in the area. What struck me this year was the front cover – but it's taken till April for me to chew over my thoughts satisfactorily.

For some people, the cover of a diocesan directory is just

a cover. For me the front cover of a diocesan directory is a bit like a record sleeve: it tells you something about the character of what you can expect inside. Record sleeves portray something about the music; the cover of a diocesan directory says something about the character of the diocese or clergy. I was therefore very interested to compare the 1996 and 1997 directory covers.

The 1996 cover showed the six-foot-tall Bishop of Birmingham, in purple robes, looking down on a very small Black girl. The Bishop is looking down questioningly, while the child, in primary-school sweatshirt, with arms on hips, gazes up at the Bishop with a puzzled look. In the background is a school building, suggesting that the Bishop has just finished leading a school assembly or is about to lead a procession out of the school. Somehow he now finds himself crossing paths with the child.

My reading of this image points to its significance. The tall Bishop, representing the might of the Anglican Church in Birmingham, signifies (to me) White, middle-class theological power. After all, the Anglican Church is mostly a suburban Church of middle-class White liberals; by contrast, its presence in the inner city is much less significant.[2] Hence, the Bishop's posture might suggest that he is lording it over the young Black child. Such imagery has a history. The annals of colonial history are littered with images of White power and domination over 'native' peoples. Hence, this 1996 image harks back to an age of colonial domination and Black subjugation.

Also significant is the Black child. She stands perplexed, unsure how to negotiate this icon of power. The frown on her face may indicate confusion or apprehension – however, she is not overwhelmed or submissive. The cover thus suggests that her gaze represents aspiration, and therefore resistance to domination. However, what is most startling about the image is her size: she is no more than five or six years old, and therefore tiny beside the bishop. If size signifies power, then it is clear who is in control here. Symbolically, I would contend that the young girl signifies the Black Anglican presence within the diocese: small, curious and problematic to those in power.

The 1997 front cover is rather different. Here, a blond grandmother and child light a candle in a church. The scene presents an image of care, concern and family bonding. Similarly, it presents the Church as a caring community, where a grandmother and child are able to participate lovingly in its life and ministry. The scene is almost reminiscent of the Madonna and Child imagery, where the viewer is drawn into the love and care between parent and child, and, more significantly, into the purity of the two characters. The two characters here also communicate a sense of purity and undefilement.

James Cone, on his 1996 visit to Queen's College, Birmingham, described hearing a family being told that the imagery of a European Jesus in an art gallery was 'ethnically accurate'. Cone mentioned the story in order to encourage his audience to make links between Christian imagery and the maintenance of White supremacy. In other words, images are deeply suggestive and have deep religio-political and ideological significance. Put simply, 'a picture paints a thousand social and political words'. If we take Cone seriously, what might be the relationship between diocesan directory covers and White Anglican supremacy in Birmingham?

In terms of power, the first image speaks volumes. White officials at every level of the organisation dominate the Diocese of Birmingham. According to a leading Black Anglican in the diocese, it has only produced a handful of Black clergy in over 40 years of ministry in Birmingham.

Is that the work of God? Likewise, in other areas of responsibility such as lay readership, Black people are underrepresented despite making up the largest group of worshippers in a significant number of inner city parishes and churches. This plantation stratification (Whites on top, Blacks on the bottom) concurs with the 1996 front cover. In sum, those with the power to produce representations of Blacks depict them as a small, problematic group.

The second image is also significant because it is a realistic ethnic projection of the heart of the Anglican Church in Birmingham. Its theology and structures emerge from and represent one particular ethnic group and social location. It is primarily a Church of the White suburb, untainted and unspoiled by the Black 'invaders'.

But there is another Birmingham not represented in either image. This is the Birmingham of rich cultural diversity and cultural crossover. A Birmingham where Black and White cultural syncretism produces new ways of interpreting life, loves and struggle. One only has to think of the structure and politics of UB40, or the African–Caribbean–Asian–British music of Apache Indian, to gain insight into this other narrative of contemporary Birmingham. In contrast, these images on the diocesan covers suggest that the Anglican Church upholds an alternative order where White is powerful, homogeneous and pure, and where Black is problematic and to be subordinated. But then again, as I said at the beginning, for some it's just a front cover.

Concluding thoughts

Several conclusions can be drawn from these four diary entries. First, that we are represented in marginal spaces – for example, there is a lack of credit given to Black gospel artists. Second, Black Christian experience is often misrepresented – we might be painted as pathological (as on the diocesan handbook's cover) or have our spirituality totally misrepresented (as in *Brothers and Sisters*). Consequently, the complex characteristics of the Black Church, and its many stories of resistance, courage, support and transformation, are ignored. Finally, negotiating and participating in popular culture requires a great deal of skill and discernment. The example of Nu Colours reveals the difficulty associated with pleasing Church and recording company.

These entries suggest that the issues confronting Black Christians are identical to those concerning Black people as a whole, as explored in a multiplicity of texts in cultural and media studies. The difference is that Black Christianity, despite being deeply influential in the lives of many Black people for many centuries, has received little, if any, meaningful analysis and exploration in popular culture, in comparison to other areas of Black life.

PART III

Theology and culture

6 Jah would never give power to a Baldhead: Bob Marley as a Black liberation theologian

The children in my family were not allowed to listen to reggae music in our house. My parents were members of the Wesleyan Holiness Church, and in the late 1970s most Wesleyans discouraged their children from listening to secular music. My parents kept strictly to this rule, and I remember many occasions when they roughly removed a reggae record which, owing to bad timing, happened to be playing on the family's stereo as they entered the living-room. My parents' dislike of secular music in general, and reggae in particular, only fed my desire for this forbidden genre. What they failed to realise was that for me, as for many of my generation, reggae music was a primary, source of historical, political and social information from Jamaica about Black history, Black culture and the state of the African diaspora. However, despite valuing reggae music, I was suspicious of Rastafari.

Black Christianity, in the form in which I experienced it, was also strongly anti-Rasta. Not only were we not allowed to listen to reggae, but we were also taught to see Rastafari as unchristian and evil. For much of my teenage life, I bought into the anti-Rasta critique of the Black Christian elders in my community; indeed, on many occasions, I publicly denounced Rastafari – despite having consumed reggae music whenever possible. Like many Christians, I was able to hold in tension, without any awareness of contradiction, a love of reggae and a dislike of Rastafari.

Today things are very different. Not only do I continue to appreciate reggae music, but I am more acutely aware of its political and religious significance in Britain. In the light of this, I want to suggest that a critical appropriation of Rastafari has much to offer the Black Church in Britain today. Reggae music offers an important theological resource for a critical reflection on Black Christianity. To support this theory, I want to explore the lyrics of Bob Marley – the canon found in his albums from 1973 to 1983 – as theological literature.

Bob Marley (1945–81) has many titles: international reggae star, global icon for Rastafari, and Jamaican musical legend. Dare we also add to this list, Bob Marley, the theologian? This depends on what we mean by 'theology'. Paul Tillich suggests that theology is the use of a 'method' to interpret the Christian faith[1] – so if we can show that Marley has a method for evaluating the Christian faith, then he is a theologian. I also want to ask two additional questions:

1. Is Bob Marley a Black liberation theologian? To be a liberation theologian, one has to be concerned with using this aforementioned method to interpret the Christian faith in the light of an oppressed community.
2. If Marley is a Black liberation theologian, what can theologians and Christians in Britain learn from him?

To answer these questions, I will begin by identifying aspects of what I consider to be Marley's method, after which I will explore the way in which his method evaluates Christianity. I will conclude by identifying ways in which Marley's theology can impact on the theology of the Black Church in Britain.

Marley's method

What then is Marley's theological method? I want to suggest two significant focuses: the first concerns the way he validates truth (that is, his system of knowing); the second concerns the way in which he interprets the Bible. We begin with his system of knowing.

Marley's knowledge-system

Naturally, Marley does not use the traditional theological methods found in your average systematic theology textbook. Instead, he draws upon three Jamaican traditions. The first is the use of experience; the second is a commitment to radical social change; and the third is the nature of the discourse, reggae music. Let us begin with experience.

For Bob Marley, experience is the basis for interpreting the social world. Consequently, he rejects the knowledge-validation processes used in the classrooms of traditional education. For Marley, traditional education is a false consciousness which maintains the subservient position of Black people. Explicit reference is made to education as false consciousness in the song *Four Hundred Years* from the *Catch a Fire* album, where The Wailers (vocals by Peter Tosh) causally link four hundred years of Black oppression with a corrupt educational system:

Four hundred years and it's the same philosophy,
Four hundred years and the people they still cannot see . . .
Four hundred years, four hundred years
Head-decay-shun and the same philosophy.

Marley's rejection of the educational system is symbolically expressed in his changing the English word 'education' to form 'head-decay-shun'. Head-decay-shun is oppression.

'Real' knowledge for Marley must be validated by experience. Experience is a filter which enables us to find meaning in the world. For instance, experience as the criterion of meaning is demonstrated in the title-song from the *Natty Dread* album. On the surface, the song describes a Rasta walking the Jamaican streets; as he walks, he hears children calling to him, sees the buildings and eventually, through these experiences, realises that Jamaica is not the home of the Rasta:

> I walked up the first street,
> And I walked up the second street to see.
> Then I trod on through third street,
> And then I call to some Dread on fourth street.
> Natty dread locks in a fifth street.
> And I skip one place to sixth street.
> I've got to reach seventh street . . .
> Oh, Oh, Natty, Natty,
> Natty twenty-one thousand miles away from home
> Oh Natty, Natty
> And that's a long way
> For Natty to be from home.

On another level, we can interpret the song as the Rasta's inner journey, the streets representing stages of consciousness. This journey entails the growing knowledge of ethnic

identity and historical belonging. So the first aspect of
Marley's method is a system of knowing built on personal
experience. But the problem with experience is that it does
not offer a more accurate means of assessing truth-claims:
experience is simply a more democratic way of approaching
the analysis of a given situation. Its primary benefit is that
it allows insight from subjugated perspectives.

The second aspect of Marley's method is commitment to
radical social change. There are two areas of concern in his
music: first, the destruction of Babylon, and second, the
liberation of the poor.

The existing social order – or 'Babylon' – must be
destroyed. As Carolyn Cooper has shown,[2] Marley advocates
both militant and psychological revolution. Regarding the
former, on several occasions Marley advocates violent
change. For example, in *Crazy Baldheads* from the album
Rastaman Vibration, he advocates noncooperation with the
system (the penal, educational and religious institutions). In
addition, 'Baldheads' – those who defend the system – must
be dealt with:

> Build your penitentiary; we build your schools
> Brain-wash education to make us the fools.
> Hate-rage you reward for our love
> Telling us of your God above.
> We gonna chase those crazy,
> Chase those crazy bunkheads,
> Chase those crazy Baldheads out of the town.

On other occasions, Marley advocates a more philosophical,
less aggressive, approach to radical social transformation.
Cooper shows that, whereas *Crazy Baldheads* talked of militant social action, *Redemption Song* on the *Uprising* album
develops the subject of psychological liberation. This song

tells Black people to free themselves from psychological oppression, referred to as 'mental slavery':

> Emancipate yourselves from mental slavery
> none but ourselves can free our minds.
> Have no fear for atomic energy
> Cause none of them can stop the time.
> How long shall they kill our prophets
> While we stand aside and look?
> Some say, 'It's just a part of it,
> We've go to fulfil the book.'
> Won't you help to sing
> These songs of freedom?
> Cause all I ever had,
> Redemption songs.

It is Marley's belief that emancipation from mental slavery is integral to liberation from social and political oppression. For example, the third line of the song, 'Have no fear for atomic energy', was written to give psychological empowerment to the African National Congress (ANC) after White apartheid South Africa had become a nuclear power. In this song, Marley wants the ANC to know that not even White nuclear power can 'stop the time' – that is, prevent the inevitability of their victory.

The second facet of Marley's commitment to radical social change is the emancipation of the poor. Marley's canon contains much creative insight into the plight of the poor, not only in Jamaica but also in Africa. He speaks with conviction of the systematic brutalisation of the weak by the powerful. However, as mentioned in the song *slave driver*, 'the table is turned'. The poor must now rise up. For example, in the song *Big Tree*, Marley proclaims that the weak and the poor, inspired by Jah, will put a halt to the work of the wicked. Marley's quest for radical social change was not realised in his lifetime – but this was not necessarily his aim. Far more important was his desire to raise the awareness of the Black masses. In this task, his contribution to Black consciousness was immense – the reason for Marley (along with several tons of amplification equipment) being the star attraction at Zimbabwe's Independence Day celebrations.

The third aspect of Marley's method is the nature of his discourse – that is, reggae music. Reggae music emerges from the urban proletariat in Jamaica. It is the descendant of slave music, containing the survivals of slave rhythms and songs. Reggae reveals how the medium in which theology is expressed is itself significant for communicating the meaning of God. In Black churches, song is a valid means of communicating divine truth – indeed, Black Pentecostalists believe that God is present in certain types of song or music. When the presence of God's Spirit is felt in a song, Black Pentecostalists talk about the music and song being 'anointed'. In a similar fashion, I am suggesting that God (Jah) may be present in the rhythms of reggae music, which expresses the aspirations of oppressed people. However, it is important to note that not all reggae is Rastafarian worship music. But our primary concern here is with 'churchical' or worship music in Rastafari.

In summary, Marley's system of knowing consists of three tools: experience, a commitment to radical social change and reggae music. Our next task is to show how this theological method interacts with the Bible. We turn to Marley's method of interpretation.

Marley's biblical interpretation

Marley's interpretive method is best understood as a process. It begins with inner revelation – truth which emerges from personal experience. In other words, when Marley says, 'So Jah seh', he refers to revelation which has come directly from Jah. Once revelation emerges, the Bible must confirm it. Guidance means finding correspondence between revelation and a biblical event, symbol or word. This exploration of the text might take place individually or communally. Reasoning with Jah is sometimes assisted by burning incense in the temple of God – that is, smoking 'ganja' (cannabis).

This hermeneutic is witnessed in the development of key doctrines. For example, the founding fathers of Rastafari believed in the deity of Haile Selassie (1892–1975 – former Emperor of Ethiopia), in Black repatriation to Africa, and that the Western world, including Jamaica, was evil. They found support for these beliefs in the Bible, and used biblical images to signify a range of correspondences with these revelations. Hence in the lyrics of Marley we discover that Selassie signifies Jah Rastafari, Africa corresponds to the Promised Land, or Zion, and Jamaica is synonymous with evil or Babylon. Marley uses this hermeneutic to interpret the contents of the Bible. I would like to demonstrate this by focusing on two of his theological hallmarks: the Second Advent of the Messiah, and Africa as the land of liberation.

The arrival of the Second Advent is declared in *Get Up, Stand Up*, on the *Burnin'* album. Marley and the Wailers confess, 'We know and we understand, the Mighty God is a living man'. Here, the 'Mighty God' is Haile Selassie. He is the Black God who has returned to save Black people. The proof of his divinity lies in Rasta's personal revelation and also biblical proof: for instance, in *Blackman Redemption*, on the *Confrontation* album, Selassie's genealogy is used as proof of his divinity: as Emperor of Ethiopia, Selassie (like Christ) is 'from the root of David, through the line of Solomon'. So just as Christians declare Jesus divine because of revelation and biblical confirmation, Marley, as a Rasta, declares Selassie divine. However, this interpretation is problematic for two reasons: first, it reveals an uncritical approach to the text; second, it relies heavily upon an idealised and romanticised view of African history.

The second theological hallmark of Bob Marley's songs is the belief that Africa – in particular, Ethiopia – is the land of liberation for Blacks. Old Testament references to Ethiopia, such as, 'Let bronze be brought from Egypt; let Ethiopia hasten to stretch out her hands to God' (Ps. 68:31), are Rastafarian proof texts which support the belief that Africa plays a central role in God's plan for Black redemption. Moreover, repatriation to Africa is seen as part of God's act of deliverance. In the title-track from the *Exodus* album, repatriation to Ethiopia is expressed as the flight of 'Jah people' to Africa. Marley asks each person to search themselves, recognise who they are and consequently leave Babylon:

> Open your eyes and look within
> Are you satisfied with the life you're living?
> We know where we're going
> We know where we're from.
> We're leaving Babylon
> We're going to our father's land.
> Exodus!
> Movement of Jah people.

Here, the personal revelation of the importance of Africa, reaffirmed in Scripture, results in a new practice: the return of Black people to Africa, psychologically as well as physically.

Is Marley a Black liberation theologian?

First, we must answer a more general question: is Marley a theologian at all? As we have seen above, Bob Marley has a theological method and applies it to the Christian Scriptures in order to produce a theology. In my opinion, Marley is a theologian – not necessarily a traditional Christian theologian but definitely a Rastafarian theologian. However, despite speaking on behalf of the marginalised and being of working-class origins, on another level, Marley must be seen and heard as a wealthy musician who maintained physical and political links with the Jamaican proletariat. In short, his perspectives, as a Rastafarian theologian, emerge from a position of relative privilege in the Jamaican context.

Second, I would contend that Marley is a Black liberation theologian, because his theology is totally concerned with the liberation of the oppressed. Nowhere is this more clearly articulated than in the final track from the *Kaya* album, entitled, *Jah would never Give Power to a Baldhead*. Here, Marley states that the work of Jah in the world is the liberation of the marginalised and downtrodden. Such is Marley's belief in God's bias towards the poor that he states categorically:

> Jah would never give power to a Baldhead
> Run come crucify the Dread
> Time alone, oh time will tell
> Think you're in heaven but you're living in hell.

Here, it is impossible for God to bless those who oppress. It is only a matter of time before divine retribution is meted out to the misguided oppressors: their heaven will become hell.

What can we learn from Marley the theologian?

We turn to our next question: if we take Marley seriously as a Black liberation theologian, what can we learn from him? I would like to outline three areas in which Marley's theology speaks to our contemporary context in Britain.

Theology and ideology

First, he informs us that theology is an ideological project – is never neutral or value-free. Like Marx, Marley believes that religion reflects human interests. In this case, Marley's ideology bespeaks local and global resistance against racialised oppression. As far as Marley is concerned, to refuse to stand up for the rights of the disenfranchised is to show a flagrant disregard for the value of human life. For example, in *Get Up, Stand Up*, on the *Burnin'* album, Marley declares to Christian people: 'If you knew what life was worth, you would fight for yours on earth'. Importantly, Marley formulates his understanding of God in the oppressed community, seeing God in the faces of the Black dispossessed.

However, we must recognise the negative ideologies in Marley's canon. Black feminist Patricia Hill Collins encourages Black thinkers to look at the lives of those people whom we deem important figures in Black communities, in order to see if their personal lives match up to their ideas. Marley's personal life raises questions for Black women, suggesting that he did not have a lot of respect for them. His promiscuous lifestyle, and his general failure to honour Black women in his music, reminds those of us concerned with using Marley as a source for our theology that any theological enterprise concerned with Black liberation in Britain must take seriously the multidimensional nature of oppression. That is, we must be not only concerned with racism but also with sexism. Given the race, class and gender exploitation of Black British women, any theology of liberation must be a theology that empowers Black women.

The African heritage

Despite Marley's highly romanticised and uncritical appropriation of Africa, there is much to gain from his focus on Africa as an area of biblical significance. Marley's Afrocentrism challenges the thrust of any Black British theology. His method suggests that our religious and cultural African roots are as important as the historical and cultural routes that make many Black people a diasporan people. This point is vitally important, especially when we consider the cultural, social, political and religious ignorance of many Black Christians in Britain concerning their African heritage. Furthermore, Marley's orientation inspires a healthy political suspicion of all theological studies and approaches which are patronising and negatively biased against Africa and Africans, both continental and diasporan. This is a real issue in theological education, where Africa and Africans are ignored in biblical studies. Only in recent years, through the efforts of Afrocentric biblical scholars and popularist writers, have Black biblical studies crept on to the syllabus of a few British theological institutions which have the vision and courage to take Black perspectives seriously. It has been interesting to note those biblical scholars who go out of their way to denigrate Black approaches to the text, despite not having read work by Afrocentric biblical scholars.[3]

Music as theology

Marley reminds us of the importance of church music as a medium for doing theology. We live at a time when many Black churches continue to borrow songs from a variety of Christian traditions, both Eurocentric and Afrocentric. It is not uncommon to go into Black churches and hear songs from traditional English hymn books, the Moody and Sankey hymnal, and Graham Kendrick. However, Marley's theology encourages us to develop a hermeneutic of suspicion towards all songs and their lyrics, because genres are political. For example, Sunday after Sunday Black Christians sing about 'lilies of the valley' and 'deer panting after water'. There is little, if any, awareness of the political and theological implications of singing about spaces and places which have very little correspondence with the real-life social spaces and places occupied by many Black and non-Black urban people. Marley encourages us to question where our songs come from, and whose world-view they articulate and validate. Another way of looking at this is to ask what kind of theology would be communicated if the images used in songs emerged from Black life-settings. Marley is an example of this process: his songs tell of his world in

Jamaica, its concrete social and political realities. This is why
I often say to the song-leaders at my church in Handsworth,
'Why don't you write a song about God in the high-rise
flats, maisonettes and housing association properties, rather
than always referring to God in hills, valleys and mansions?
Surely God belongs in our neighbourhood too?' What I am
suggesting is a relocation of songs and lyrics to facilitate a
more vivid expression of God's presence among us.

Marley's theology and Christianity

Possibly the most challenging aspect of Marley's theology
is its diametric opposition to traditional Christianity. By
proclaiming that 'Jah would never give power to a Baldhead', on the *Kaya* album, Marley rejects the authority of
Baldhead religion, that is, Christianity.[4] Marley experiences
European Christianity as an integral part of the *rhaatid*
(English-raging)[5] Babylon system. Furthermore, the European–Christian collusion in slavery, colonialism, imperialism
and neo-colonialism in Jamaica is proof of its inherent anti-
Blackness. Hence, for Marley, Black people cannot achieve
their God-given humanity within the Christian religion. To
do so, they must become Rastafarian.

However, this is a contradiction. Although Rastafari
claims to be qualitatively different from European theology,
in reality Rastafari is bound to the traditional English–
Christian religion, because it uses the same manuscript traditions and sources. Despite this aberration, Marley
challenges us to question the usefulness of the Christian
religion for Black diasporan subjects – namely, how can we
reconstruct the Baldhead religion so that it has relevance in

contemporary Black Britain? As mentioned above, when reconstructing Baldhead religion, we must take seriously Black women's (womanist) concerns about patriarchy in Black Christianity.

Marley's theology continues to live in the appropriations of Black diasporan music; it is highly significant that, for many weeks in the charts recently, the Number 1 song was *Killing Me Softly* by the versatile, highly politicised US hard-core hip-hop trio The Fugees, who claim Bob Marley as their primary musical influence.[6] In tribute, like many musicians worldwide, they rework his social and political critique and religious orientation. Hence, through The Fugees, another generation of listeners and consumers are exposed to Marley, whose theology points us to a God of rhythm, in tune with the rhythms of Black life.

7 Jesus is Dread: language and Christology

The value of culture as an element of resistance to
foreign domination lies in the fact that culture is the
vigorous manifestation on the ideological plane of
the physical and historical reality of the society that is
dominated or to be dominated. Culture is simultaneously the fruit of a people's history, by the positive
or negative influence which it exerts on the evolution
of the relationship between man/*woman* and his/*her*
environment, among men/*women* or groups of men/
women within society, as well as different societies.
Ignorance of this fact may explain the failure of several
attempts at foreign domination – as well as the failure
of some liberation movements.

(Amical Cabral – my additions in italics)

Is it possible to be a Black Pentecostal Christian and Black
conscious – concerned with Black socio-political mobilisation in Britain today? This question expresses a concern of
many young, second and third generation Black Pentecostal
Christians in Britain, for whom the type of Black Pentecostalism brought by their parents from the Caribbean was or
is politically quietist.[1] Growing up in the 1970s and 1980s,
I witnessed two forms of political quietism: spiritualisation
and pacification.

By 'spiritualisation', I mean the way in which the actual,
real-life concerns of the Black community, and indirectly of
the Black Church, were interpreted as cosmic concerns

only to be changed by consulting God through prayer. Consequently, if family security was threatened by a racist attack, our most effective response was prayer. We believed that God would fight our battles, and after long, sincere and dynamic family or church prayer-sessions, we not only felt better but believed that God had heard and was dealing with our interests. Racism was not explicitly mentioned, but was sometimes implicit in our prayers. Despite the psycho-social satisfaction we experienced from prayer, this spiritualisation of reality promoted socio-political passivity: there was no external protest or challenge to the White supremacist powers within our town.

By 'pacification', I mean our commitment to a particular domestic, neo-colonial social mentality whereby we responded to oppression with dignity, pride and self-respect. For example, my father was intimidated and bullied by the local police force when they stopped and searched his car for no reason. Faced with this situation, rather than expressing his anger verbally and possibly violently, he responded in the opposite way. Calmly and with dignity he answered their questions and showed the appropriate documents. He believed that, by not displaying anger, he had shown the police that he was above intimidation and had 'won a moral victory'. This type of passive socio-political response to our existential concerns was related to our faith in a God of order, who governed our behaviour. Consequently we did not engage in social analysis – and we certainly did not think about political action.

Juxtaposing these family experiences with the praxis of Black consciousness, occurring within the African–Caribbean British community in the 1970s and early 1980s, reveals a dialectical tension: Black consciousness opposed the political quietism of my parents and our Black Pentecostal Church tradition.

British Black consciousness movements of the 1970s and early 1980s, as social and political philosophies, were concerned with Black empowerment by means of three developments: cultural appreciation, social and historical recovery, and collective political action.[2] First, cultural appreciation meant taking Black culture seriously in a context where the appreciation and development of Blackness was oppositional both politically and socially. Cultural appreciation was an inherent feature of the Rastafari movement in the 1970s.

Second, social and historical recovery meant the excavation and recontextualisation of Black traditions of emancipation. These traditions and perspectives were considered hidden from the consciousness of Black peoples by centuries of European hegemony. In the 1970s and 1980s, social and historical recovery was manifest in the explosion in the number of Black newspapers and publishing houses, all concerned with developing community identity, and Black psychological and social development, through strategies of self-love and self-respect. Third, political action as a component of Black consciousness was concerned with self-mobilisation and group-mobilisation – that is, the emancipation of the Black community from oppressive forces, such as structural racism and unemployment. It involved activities such as political education (decolonisation) and political mobilisation (marches, Saturday schools, boycotts, etc.). In the 1970s and 1980s the growth of independent Black political organisations, political parties and numerous Black women's groups, as well as Black gay and lesbian action movements, typifies the political action of this period.

However, it would be wrong to assume that the tensions between Black British Pentecostal faith (as expressed in spiritualisation and pacification) and Black consciousness, as identified above, are irreconcilable. There are schools of

thought that present the Black Church movement in Britain
as a form of Black resistance. Such scholars look at the
establishment, proliferation and consolidation of Black
Churches in the midst of White oppression in Britain as a
form of Black resistance – a conscious attempt to resist
oppression. Valentina Alexander and Roswith Gerloff argue
this view.

First, Alexander suggests that the Black Church movement displays resistance in two forms. These are passive and
active radicalism:

> The notable feature of passive radicalism is that whilst
> it is often encouraged within a collective context, for
> example through communal worship or Bible study
> etc., it is, nonetheless, meant to serve the practical
> interests of the individual believer. It gives them the
> strength and incentive to cope with the ideological and
> material disadvantages which confront them . . . Active
> radicalism is so called because whilst emanating from
> the same source as passive radicalism, it nonetheless
> attempts a more systematic and, above all, corporate
> attack against the oppression experience . . . to chal-
> lenge and eventually dismantle the structures of society
> from which oppression is manifested and maintained.[3]

Alexander's passive/active dichotomy draws upon the sur-
vival/liberation paradigm of Black Christian faith found in
the work of the African–American historian, Gayraud
Wilmore. Significantly, Alexander eventually states that
active radicalism has 'not been fully authenticated by the
main body of leadership' within most of the Black
Churches. Hence, her analysis suggests that the horizons of
Black Pentecostal faith and Black consciousness intersect –
but would do so most clearly in active radicalism.

Second, Roswith Gerloff, a scholar of the Black British Church movement, identifies an equivalent theme in the Black Church to that of Alexander's active radicalism. Gerloff's analysis of the Apostolic Movement (i.e. the Jesus only church tradition) in the Caribbean and Britain leads her to conclude that, as a Black religio-cultural movement, uplifting, guiding and restoring Black people, the Black Church functions as a form of 'Christian Black power'.[4]

Alexander is closer to the truth of the situation: most Black Church traditions come into the category of passive radicalism. In contrast, Gerloff's statement appears a gross exaggeration, especially when the Black Church's political analysis is placed alongside Black nationalist traditions in Britain – such as the Black Panthers, Race Today Collective, Rastafari and the Nation of Islam. So a large vacuum still exists between the Black Church and Black consciousness – or passive and active radicalism.

This vacuum is the concern of this chapter – more specifically, the political and ideological distance between survival and liberation in Black British Christianity. Those within the Church who are concerned with a holistic Black liberation must find a theology which takes seriously engagement with the social and political world. Such a theology must find a way to reconcile Black Christian faith with Black consciousness, in order to move beyond a theology of survival towards a theology of liberation.[5] I would like to suggest that one way of reconciling what I perceive as antithetical but interrelated responses to Black oppression is to use aspects of Black culture to reflect criti-cally on Black Christianity. Obviously there are other ways of unlocking the passivity of the Black Church, but culture is significant for several reasons. First, for a long time the African diaspora in the Caribbean, and now in Britain, has mobilised culture as a form of resistance to White oppression.[6] Second, the adoption of aspects of Black expressive culture by Black Christians is not a new phenomenon in Black Christian circles – for generations, Black Christians have selectively appropriated aspects of Black popular culture in order to enhance and enrich Black faith. Church music and dress-styles are two examples. Third, it is not an anomaly for Black Christians to make political and ideological capital out of mobilising Black culture. For example, the introduction of 'curly perm' hair-styles in the 1980s in Black Churches did much to demarcate social and ideological boundaries between conservative and liberal Black Christians. Initially, for some having a curly perm was an act of rebellion against the conservative aesthetics of many churches.

I want to stretch the boundaries, and suggest a form of cultural borrowing which draws from radical aspects of Black culture in order to construct a more radical Black British Christian faith. This suggestion requires clarification.

I propose to show that there are distinctive elements of resistance embedded within Black popular culture – elements which can be used to reflect critically upon the faith and praxis of the Black Churches in Britain. In short, I want to correlate radical elements of Black popular culture with elements of Black Church culture to form the basis for reflection on aspects of Black theology. I hope that this process will help us in developing a revolutionary theology concerned with socio-political liberation.

There are three aspects to this quest. First, I will define some of the characteristics of Black British culture in order to identify its radicality. Second, I will search for an appropriate framework for facilitating a critical dialogue between popular culture, Church culture and Black Christian faith. Finally, I will attempt to identify the consequences of the dialogue between culture and Black Christian faith by exploring its implications for theology, in particular Christology.

1   The characteristics of Black British culture

What do we mean when we talk about Black culture? The 'Black' component of Black culture is difficult to define. Stuart Hall suggests that it is located within those Black communities where the experience of struggle against oppression and resistance to it produces distinctive 'cultural repertoires' from which popular representations emanate.

For Hall, this communal–organic understanding, while avoiding essentialism, defines and authenticates Black popular cultures. Furthermore, he outlines three expressive repertoires within Black culture which signify its difference or otherness. The first concerns style: in Black popular culture, style is not a mere veneer or coating, but is itself the subject. Second, Black popular culture is deeply attached to music, in contrast to mainstream culture's logocentric commitment to the written word.[7] Third, the body is intentionally used as canvas (this means that the style of dress or hair design are artistic expressions on the Black body). Here, I am concerned with the form and relationship of these expressions in Britain. Studies suggest that Black cultural expression is influenced and reshaped by experience, syncretism, plurality and ideology.

Culture and experience

As mentioned by Hall, Black culture is intimately related to experience. To say that cultural expression is central to experience is to see Black culture as the creation of the concrete experience of being Black. Examples of this inter-relatedness of culture and experience can be found in studies on the relationship between Jamaican society and the emergence of reggae culture, and between the Civil Rights Movement and the development of Soul culture in North America.[8]

The organic relationship between experience and culture is taken seriously in Black theology, where culture is mobilised as a form of resistance. The relationship between culture, experience and Black resistance has a long history. As Theo Smith shows, the African diaspora merged African-derived practices with Euro-Christian sources and traditions to produce a distinctive culture of 'conjuration' which was the basis of Black resistance in the New World.[9] Black theologian James Cone echoes this view, arguing that Black culture is the creative response of Black people trying to 'carve out an existence in dehumanised White society'.[10]

In the UK context, the relationship between experience, culture and resistance in Black Church circles is witnessed in the symbolic names given to churches in Britain, particularly within the Black Apostolic tradition. Church-names such as Bethel, Beulah and Shiloh were used by post-war Caribbean migrants to Britain as signifiers of places of refuge in a hostile world.[11]

Culture and syncretism

Second, Black expressive culture is not static but syncretistic –
in other words, it is in dialogue with various other cultures
and is therefore promiscuous in the sense that it mixes
without restraint. The dialogue between Black and White
cultures has received a great deal of critical analysis because
Black/White syncretism is a feature of most Black diasporan
communities.[12] In contrast, here I want to consider examples
of lateral exchanges between Black diasporan communities,
particularly between Jamaica, Britain and the USA. This
'golden triangle' has had a profound effect upon Black
Church life in Britain. Moreover, according to Black British
cultural critic Kobena Mercer, cultural fusion is one way in
which Black communities develop ways of 'surviving and
thriving in conditions of crisis and transition'.[13] I cite, as
examples in Britain, the emergence of African–Caribbean
British reggae, rap and gospel genres in the 1970s, 1980s
and 1990s.

The fusion of Jamaican musical styles with Black British
culture produced a distinctive Black British reggae, exempli-
fied by the bands Steel Pulse and Aswad. For example, Steel
Pulse's first album, *Handsworth Revolution*, reworks Jamaican
reggae's tradition of melodic, lyrical construction as well as
its criticism of capitalism and racism – but in the context
of race and racism in Britain, and the Black struggle here.[14]
Likewise, when Aswad sing their classic track, *African
Children*, in high-rise, inner-city housing projects, they refer
to a particular Black British diasporan experience:

> African Children, living in a concrete situation,
> African Children,
> They don't know where you're coming from,
> African Children.[15]

In these cases, Handsworth and Brixton are in need of liberation. But it is Trench Town, Jamaica, which provides the musical style and critical insight necessary for the remoulding of this genre in Britain.

A more recent example of the continuing interface between Black expressive cultures within the diaspora can be seen in the evolution of the rap genre. The entry of Black sound-systems from Jamaica, with their stylistic lyrical commentary or 'toasting' over reggae music's dub sound-tracks, inspired African–Americans to appropriate this style and produce their own interpretation, called rap. Further recontextualisation in Britain completed rap's historic journey to England.

Finally, the cultural expressions of the Black Church in Britain are also subject to syncretism. This exchange has a long history. Black-on-Black theological exchanges started with the arrival of free Black preachers travelling from the USA to spread a Black gospel tradition to Black slaves in the Caribbean in the eighteenth century.[16] This diaspora interchange is evident today in Black British Church culture – for example, the influence of African–American Church culture in Britain and Jamaica found in gospel music and Black preaching. Both formats are deeply indebted to cultural borrowing from the African–American tradition.

Contemporary African–Caribbean British gospel groups – such as The Wades and Nu Colour and the likes of Paradise before them – appropriate styles from African–American gospel music to produce distinctive British gospel sounds. Similarly, Black British ministers mix African–American accents with Caribbean British Creole to augment the spirituality of their oral discourse. Many Black Christians pray in Caribbean Creoles, speak in English and preach in American accents. In the early 1980s, the coalescence of these Black Atlantic gospel traditions was reflected in a Channel 4 TV gospel show, *People, Get Ready!* This programme played host to both British and American gospel artists, uniting a common tradition of using church music as a form of spiritual uplift and social commentary.

Culture and plurality

Because Black culture is syncretistic, it is also a plural culture. Black plurality means that we can no longer speak of one distinctive, homogeneous Black British experience or singular cultural identity. Therefore, attempts to unify the Black experience by asserting cultural homogeneity ignore the multilayered voices which are inherent within Black communities. Victor Anderson, in *Beyond Ontological Blackness*, mentions this concern in relation to Black theology, arguing that we must move beyond an ontological Blackness which essentialises Black experience. Instead, he posits a postmodern Blackness in which Blackness recognises the continual reconstruction of Black identities and Black cultures in diasporan contexts.[17]

Black Christian experience is also plural. As we saw in the Introduction, we cannot talk about Black Christianity as a singular experience. Similarly the traditional division of Black Christian experience into the two neat categories – Black majority and White majority, or Black-led and White-led – is exploded by the presence of Black Christians in charismatic house churches, independent White Churches, independent new-wave Black Churches and independent multiracial Churches. The singular Black Christian experience is now legion.

Culture and ideology

Culture is ideological – that is, cultural repertoires can be used to construct cultural systems which signify particular meanings in social and political arenas. For example, in Britain, many Rastafarians still wear dreadlocks in a symbolic identification with their African past, identifying themselves as representatives of mental decolonisation and defenders of the cultural and political interests of the Black community. In contrast, cultural systems may also be used to legitimise 'internalised oppression'. The African–American philosopher Cornel West, for example, has identified nihilistic tendencies within contemporary African–American culture, particularly, the emergence of West Coast gangster rap in the late 1980s. According to West's analysis, cultural systems are mobilised to legitimise misogyny, homophobia and lateral (i.e. Black-on-Black) violence.[18]

The notion of cultural ideology is important because the idea of culture as resistance is used by Black theologians. Black theology identifies the liberating cultural traditions within the Black community which provide the necessary strength for resistance. For example, in *The Spiritual and the Blues*, Cone identifies the political and ideological strands within Negro spirituals.[19] Similarly, in the UK context, Carol Tomlin has identified the cultural ideologies present in Black preaching in Britain.[20]

In summary, Black cultural repertoires do not occur in a vacuum. Culture is hotly contested and is an ideological battleground. How then does it function as a source for the development of a theology of liberation for the Black Church in Britain? In a more extensive study we could examine the theological significance of cultural syncretism, plurality and experience – for example, the way in which cultural plurality can encourage the Black Church to take seriously the polyphony within the Black community. The voices of Black women, the poor, and gay and lesbians all offer insights into Black existence – and all of these are needed to engage critically with the way in which we do theology. In short, God's prophetic voice is not confined to your average Black church.

However, I will focus here on ideology. I would like to explore the way in which seeing culture as resistance can affect our appraisal of Black theology. It is first necessary to construct an appropriate framework for facilitating a critical dialogue between culture as ideology (resistance) and one aspect of theology – Christology.

2   A framework for critical dialogue

As mentioned above, the Black Church and Black consciousness are at odds: they choose alternative ways of negotiating Black life in Britain. This is what Stuart Hall calls the 'ideological negotiation of resistance'[21] – in other words, Black resistance in every context is varied, subjective and diverse. However, one way of building an ideological and political bridge between the Black Church and Black consciousness is to view the organic relationship between these two traditions: we can see the Black Church as the soil in which the seeds of a more explicit Black consciousness can grow. In other words, I am suggesting that the liberating cultural system external to the Church can be the catalyst enabling strands of cultural resistance to exist within the Black Church. This process can result in new theological reflection within the Black Church. We thus have two tasks: first to identify the systems of cultural resistance in Black Church culture; second, to identify a catalyst to enable the move from cultural resistance to culture as liberation in the Black Church.

Resistance within the Black Church

There are several areas in which the Black Church move- ment exhibits cultural resistance – such as gospel music[22] and church dress.[23] However, here I would like to focus on Creole language or Black-talk.

Cultural resistance exists within the Black Church in the persistence of Black-talk. The Black Church in Britain has been one of the few social spaces in which Black people can gather and experience the expressiveness of Black lan- guage. For example, when I was growing up in Britain during the 1970s, the church was the only place, apart from home, where Black-talk was acceptable and fully used with all its stylistic devices. The maintenance and development of Creole within the Church is a form of resistance on two levels. First, it provides a vocabulary and language in which Black people can share their struggles and collectively stand in solidarity without the need to talk White – talking White brings a sense of non-being to many people of the Carib- bean diaspora. Second, Black-talk is Black creative expression. Take, for example, Black prayer styles where prayer is a rich tapestry of song, exaltation and intercession. Some would argue that Black prayer is at its best when extemporaneous, corporate and polemical. The expressive language of this prayer tradition is undergirded by a par- ticular psychological history: Black-talk was a means of affirming self-worth in the midst of slavery and colonial oppression. When used in the Church, Black-talk becomes a theological matter: speaking to God in Creole suggests that God is a Creole speaker too. Hence, Black-talk reflects God's participation in Black existence – and praying in the Black Church with passion and expression is a divine affirmation of Black self-worth.

From resistance to liberation

If the Black Church embodies elements of cultural resistance, how can it move from a culture of resistance to a culture of liberation? I propose a solution which makes use of Black-talk in the Black Church, by importing and reworking a linguistic term (catalyst) from Black popular culture which communicates liberation; I shall then use it to reflect on Christology.

The term is 'Dread' – a term which emerged with the Rastafarian movement in the Caribbean. Rastafarians *invert* the traditional English usage of 'dread', so that rather than meaning fear and anxiety, Dread means upliftment, freedom and empowerment. Rastafarians wore dreadlocks to symbolise the process of mental decolonisation, freedom, power and upliftment. Despite the decline of Rastafari as a movement in Britain today, Dread culture is still present, reconfigured in Black popular culture, where it continues to play an integral role in Black cultural resistance.[24]

Politically, Dread is concerned with rebellion. In terms of aetiology, Dread signified freedom from oppression. Originally Rastas were concerned with the anti-colonial struggle – but the concept of Dread now goes beyond Rastafari and is a common expression among Black and White people in Britain. Even so, the term is still used to suggest that which is good and meaningful within the lives of Black people. To call someone or something Dread is to recognise a certain dynamism. Socially, the concept Dread has many meanings – for example, it is used in the concept of 'funki dreads', a music and cultural movement outside Rastafari in Britain. Similarly, there exists a multiracial pop group called Dread Zone. Dread culture today is thus represented in a variety of cultural expressions and under various titles. My concern here is to use the political meaning of Dread to rethink Christology.

3   Dread and Christology

What happens when the term Dread is applied to Christology? In other words, what happens when we use a linguistic term, which has the resonances described above, to reflect on Black Christian theology, in particular, on Christology? To answer the question, we must investigate two issues. First, Christology and second, hermeneutics.

Christology

Christology is not concerned here with European christological formulations as expressed in the Nicene or Chalcedonian creeds. Instead, Christology considers what it means for Jesus to be the Christ for oppressed people in Britain: a Black Christology must underpin the dual task of resisting systems of White supremacy, as well as developing a political and social structure which is capable of challenging the domestic, neo-colonial situation faced by Black

British people. I suggest that we begin by calling Jesus Dread.

Naming Jesus Dread uses the power of Black-talk in the Black Church, where language is used symbolically as a form of empowerment. This is the point of correlation between Black consciousness and the traditions of resistance within the Black Church. Language is a powerful means of producing a change in thought and action. The transforming power of language is expressed in the structural linguistics of Ferdinand de Saussure, who sees symbolic language as a signifier, conveying a hidden meaning.[25] Similarly, Jung suggests that all symbols have a 'wider unconsciousness' which leads to other ideas beyond us.[26] Finally, regarding the symbolic function of theological language, Paul Tillich suggests that language can be understood as an ontological symbol.[27] Ontological symbols are used to point us to the divine, using limited human language to describe the infinite being we call God. For Tillich, ontological symbols point beyond us, and participate in that reality, as well as unlocking truths about God and human beings. Consequently, to talk of a Dread Christ points us to a Christ of faith who participates in the struggles for Black freedom.

What then are the hallmarks of a Dread Christ? A Dread Christ equips Black folk to face and destroy all structures of oppression – being Dread, for the Black Church, is to engage in the struggle for Black freedom. Furthermore, to say that Christ is Dread is to unveil a Christ of Black upliftment, Black empowerment and Black progress. Similarly, a Dread Christ tells Black British people that the Jesus of history is with them as they protest, fight, boycott, celebrate and progress. In short, a Dread Christ is a Black Christ participating in Black lives and Black struggles. In the context of Britain, a Dread Christ is the focus of our

socio-political struggle and the source of joy for our resur-
rected lives.

Hermeneutics

The second issue we need to explore is what happens if we
make the Dread Christ the norm, or the hermeneutical
paradigm, by which we do theology in the Black Church.
In my opinion, the Dread Christ provides us with an opportunity for developing a theology of Black liberation. But in
order for the Dread Christ to become an interpretative
norm, we must ensure that it functions as a 'new hermeneutic'.

Liberation theology in Latin America has taught those
struggling for justice to explore hermeneutical procedures
which relocate the production of theology within the locus
of the experience of the oppressed. By giving experience a
more weighty epistemological value, liberation theologians
argue that we are more likely to find a hermeneutic which
relates to the life-setting of oppressed people. In other
words, the experiences of Black people in Britain become
our primary text. This should not mean that we invert the
power-relations so that Black experience is elevated, is made
supreme. Instead, the relocation of theology provides a more
democratic approach to assessing what and who Jesus is in
the world today.

As mentioned above, Blackness is not homogeneous – it
is multifaceted and diverse. Hence, as a Black man, with
particular theological presuppositions, and social and
political perspectives, I can only speak with integrity and
honesty about my context and my liberation. My hope is
that, by and through the Spirit, these concerns will resonate

with second and third generation Black Christians in similar situations and circumstances. In other words, this process of developing a new hermeneutic is partial and limited. Moreover, without the involvement and engagement of other voices, especially those concerned with issues of gender and sexuality, my own hermeneutic will lack a truly radical and holistic dimension. Even so, I present my argument as one voice alongside others 'crying out loud in the wilderness'.

How then do we develop the Dread Christ as a hermeneutical norm? I begin with J. L. Segundo, who, in *The Liberation of Theology*, identifies four distinct stages in the development of the hermeneutics of liberation:

1. taking seriously our real-life experience;
2. the need for analysis;
3. a new way of doing theology;
4. a new hermeneutic.[28]

Applying this hermeneutical procedure in the context of Black Britain provides us with some insights into how we can develop a new hermeneutic related to the Black British quest for justice.

First, taking our experience seriously means that we must engage with the struggle against racism and against the ideological White supremacy in Britain. Liturgy and church life must identify and challenge the psychologically damaging effects of White supremacy, and must also engage in the Black community's struggle for political mobilisation. For example, Black Churches cannot continue to sing songs which portray an oppressive, Eurocentric reality and community – particularly when these images do damage to the Black psyche as mentioned above. Given the negative evaluation of Blackness, can Black people concerned with

LION OF JUDAH

Lion of Judah by Robert Lentz (1988)
©Robert Reck

The Last Supper I by Faisal Abduallah (1995)

The Last Supper II by Faisal Abduallah (1995)

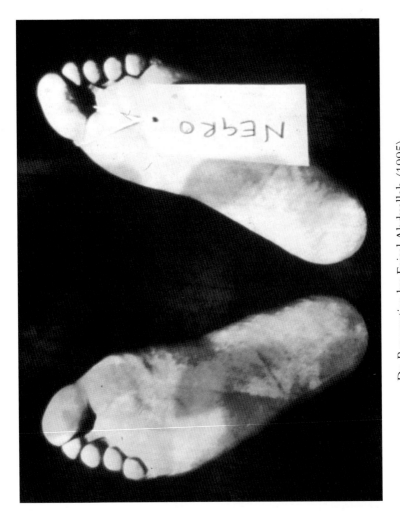

Da Resurrection by Faisal Abduallah (1995)

Black liberation continue to sing, 'Lord, wash me and I shall be whiter than snow'? Likewise, the Black Church must end the conspiracy of silence, and engage in dialogue with Black politics – particularly with the political groups which are developing strategies for Black mobilisation. In other words, the Church must sit down and 'break bread' and critically engage with Black nationalists in Britain. Theologically, developing a Dread Christology will assist this process by representing Christ as incarnate within Black people's struggle for justice, thereby proclaiming to the Black community the Church's commitment to Black struggle. In other words, a Dread Christ must communicate the revolutionary message of what it means to overturn the forces which desire the non-existence of the Black community.

Second, this new hermeneutic must involve analysis to unlock the complexity of the Black condition. On the one hand, Black oppression in Britain is rooted in the maintenance of systems of White supremacy. One cure requires a psychological conversion within the Black community. The Black Church can assist the process of mental decolonisation by debunking the myth of colour-blindness rooted in the claim that theology is neutral and therefore universal. A Dread theology must debunk this myth by asserting the ideological nature of theology: all theology is ideological – it is either siding with, or working on behalf of, a particular group.

On the other hand, ideological analysis must ensure that we also investigate and identify Black diversity. Despite the emphases of this chapter, Black life consists of more than simply resisting oppression: Black people in Britain are diverse, and located in numerous social spaces carving out numerous identities and strategies for existence. This dimension of Black life must also be an issue for analysis. In other words, we must encourage analysis of the theological meaning and socio-political implications of Black diversity in Britain. Armed with this ideological suspicion, we must reapproach the process of doing theology.

Third, we must reappropriate Black experience and history as relevant sources for a new Black theology in Britain. Rather than looking to Luther, Calvin, Wesley or Tomlinson (founder of the New Testament Church of God), we must re-engage with our history, re-investigating the ministry and philosophy of the rebel leaders of the Caribbean in the last century – for example, Nanny of the Maroons, Paul Bogel and William George Gordon of the Morant Bay Rebellion (1865), the rebellion of Samuel Sharp (Jamaica, 1832) and the politics and spirituality of the nineteenth-century Jamaican Baptist mystic, Anthony Bedward. Similarly we must re-engage with the radical messages of the early pan-African E. W. Blyden, and the forerunners of Black nationalism Amy and Marcus Garvey, as well as asking forgiveness for 'closing our ears' to the prophetic voice within Rastafari. Unlike the apostle Paul, we must listen to the Spirit calling us to go south, rather than being solely preoccupied with the intellectual traditions of the north. Consequently, we must permit our social locations to determine the questions that theology must answer. Black people want to know what God is doing about their situation: Black unemployment, racism in education, business progress and the criminal justice system.

Finally, through this new approach to theology we arrive at a new hermeneutical principle: the Black Christ is with us as we strive for freedom against the forces of oppression.

Beyond the Dread Christ

As mentioned above, the remnants of Dread culture remain, in recontextualised forms, in Black popular culture in Britain. Even so, we must recognise the limitations of dreadness. First, Dread as a concept is time-bound and in some sense, *passé*. So it is necessary to find new ways of talking about Christ and the work of God in Black communities – ways which take us beyond Dread. For example, we must note the cultural significance of the emergence of post-nationalist movements in Britain, as well as the contextualisation of Afrocentrism in the Black British context. In short, we must ask whether British hip-hop or the multicultural, hybrid forms of jungle music can provide us with new ways of challenging Church culture, and therefore theology. In other words, how do these genres affiliate and disaffiliate with the narratives of resistance found in Dread culture? Also, Dread as a concept is underpinned by Black, masculinist presuppositions: Dread emerges from the contexts of resistance of Black men in the Caribbean and its diaspora in Britain. Therefore Dread must be critiqued by Black feminist and other voices, to challenge the patriarchal and hegemonic tendencies of a Dread Christology.

Returning to my question at the beginning of this chapter: is it possible to be a Black Pentecostal Christian and Black conscious? The answer is a resounding Yes. A correlation of the revolutionary aspirations of the Black community found in Dread culture with the resistance of the Black Church is one way of producing a theology which seriously engages with Black consciousness in Britain. Moreover, while the Black Church is a survival institution at a time when more than a passive response is possible from Black Church, not to develop strategies of liberation is to validate our own oppression. A Church that refuses to speak

to and represent the Black quest for freedom is a Church
that continues to belong to the slavemaster.

8 Sisters in the house: the emergence and challenge of womanist theology in Britain

Womanist, from womanish (opp. of 'girlish,' i.e., friv-
olous, irresponsible, not serious.) A Black feminist or
feminist of colour. From the Black folk-expression of
mothers to female children, 'You acting womanish,'
i.e., like a woman. Usually referring to outrageous,
audacious, courageous or wilful behaviour. Wanting to
know more and in greater depth than is considered
'good' for one. Interest in grown-up doings. Acting
grown up. Interchangeable with another Black folk-
expression: 'You trying to be grown.' Responsible. In
charge. Serious.
(Alice Walker)

Womanist theology begins with the experiences of
Black women as its point of departure. This experience
includes not only Black women's activities in the larger
society but also in the churches, and reveals that Black
women have often rejected the oppressive structure in
the church as well. These experiences provide a
context, which is significant for doing theology. Those
experiences have been and continue to be defined by
racism, sexism and classism and therefore offer a unique
opportunity and a new challenge for developing a relevant perspective in the theological enterprise. This
perspective in theology which I am calling womanist

theology draws upon the life and experiences of some
Black women who have created meaningful interpre-
tations of the Christian faith.
(Jacquelyn Grant)

Go into any Black church anywhere in the country and
you will see that the Black Church in Britain is primarily
female – in the sense that women dominate numerically.
Unfortunately, numerical superiority does not always mean
having equal status or power to men – as mentioned in
Chapter 1, the Black Church is guilty of sexism. However,
the role of women in the Church is a complex one. While
under-represented in positions of leadership, Black women
have been able to find ways of making their voices heard
and of directing the Church, despite Black male dominance
(patriarchy). Another way of describing this situation is to
say that, for a variety of reasons, Black women take a back
seat in the Church but still remain in the driving seat. While
this suggestion identifies a more complex resistance by Black
women, it does not account for the numerous situations
and circumstances in which Black women have been
silenced and dismissed because Black men, in particular,
have not seen them as equal to themselves in the sight of
God.

Theological justification for female inferiority – the
notion that women are the 'weaker vessel' – is theologically
and historically weak. Theologically the notion is based
upon the premise that the Bible must be translated word-
for-word into today's Church. Many Black Churches still
quote as law the Pauline text which limited the role of
women in the Church and home. Such a viewpoint encourages many men to use the Bible to condemn the behaviour
of women, especially behaviour which is deemed to
endanger the spiritual purity of men. Rarely is the Bible

used in a similar manner to challenge men. For example, the Bible is seldom used to encourage Black churchmen to be moderate in dress and demeanour – a brother in a nice suit is equated with spiritual blessing and masculine potency. By contrast, a sister in a beautifully tailored dress or outfit is likely to be considered wanton rather than sophisticated. When the Bible is used in this manner, it reflects the fears of men rather than the inspiration of God.

The notion that women are inferior to men is also weak historically. The history of the Black Church in Britain shows that it is fundamentally a women's movement. Every Black church in Britain has a plethora of 'mothers' who have been, or who are, instrumental in the teaching, evangelism, fund-raising, prayer life, preaching, cleaning, cooking, care-taking and the general well-being of the church. For example, my mother, Naomi Louise Beckford, has pioneered the development of two churches among the Caribbean diaspora during her time in England. On each occasion she began by holding meetings of the Wesleyan Holiness Church in the front room of our house. Planting and running a church is no easy matter – and is made even harder while raising a large family in a patriarchal household and doing a full-time job. Even now, at sixty-nine, she is planning a move to another city in order to start 'new work' for the Lord! The example of my mother, and many other church 'mothers', suggests that it is nonsense to suggest that Black women have been a secondary influence in the proliferation and development of Black churches in Britain. In reality, they have been central to this work. Unfortunately, many of the most recent studies have failed to acknowledge this fact.[1]

In recent years, the emergence of womanist theology on the African–American theological scene has corrected the limited awareness of Black women's lives within the Church.

Womanists have written critiques of sexism, and also frame-
works for a theology which takes seriously the struggles and
achievements of Black women. Womanist theology is an
attempt to articulate the theological concerns of Black
women. Although it is a complex tradition, there are several
tools employed by womanists which provide insight into its
nature.

The tools of womanism

There are four distinct tools used by womanist theologians.
First, there is mobilisation of historical memory. Womanist
theologians scour the historical record for models of Black
women who provide inspiration and direction for Black
women's social and political concerns today. For example,
womanist theologians in the African–American context have
drawn inspiration and direction from historical figures such
as Harriet Tubman, Sojourner Truth, Zora Neal Hurston
and Ida B. Wells-Barnett.[2] Similarly, Black women in the
Bible, such as Hagar and the Queen of Sheba, receive similar
attention.[3] This reappropriation of Black heroines has been
subject to criticism from Black male scholars – in particular,
Victor Anderson, who has argued that these attempts to
valorise historical figures fails to acknowledge the lessons
which must be learned from less heroic and more tragic
figures in Black life. He cites the work of novelist Toni
Morrison as an alternative framework for mobilising the
historic memory, because of her willingness to make sense
out of what is grotesque in Black life.[4]

Second, womanist theologians have developed alternative
ways of evaluating what we 'know'. Validating knowledge

is important because, if Black women's knowledge about
life is defined and evaluated, it can better resource Black
women's resistance and achievement. A good example of a
womanist knowledge-validation process occurs in the work
of Black feminist Patricia Hill Collins. Collins contrasts the
contemporary knowledge-validation processes in academic
institutions with that of Black women. She shows that Black
women in the diaspora have constructed, from their African
past, mutual struggles and safe spaces – an alternative knowledge-validation system. This validation system makes use of
Black women's experience, the empathy of dialogue, the
measure of personal accountability and an ethic of caring.[5]
These tools offer an anti-domination knowledge-validation
process (what she calls a counter-hegemonic epistemology).
The articulated wisdom traditions and knowledge sources
of Black women provide a more democratic approach to
understanding what is really 'true' in the world today.

Third, womanists use a multidimensional analysis, which
seeks a broad understanding of marginalisation, to unlock
the condition of Black women. Whereas Black theology
tends to focus on issues of race and class marginalisation,[6]
womanists take seriously class, race, gender and sexuality.[7]
This approach enables an understanding of interlocking
systems of oppression which restrict the lives of Black
women. While all Black women do not suffer marginalisation in the same way, multidimensional analysis seeks to
identify structural forces which restrict the lives of the most
deprived and ostracised within the community. One
important aspect of multidimensional analysis is the
boundary placed upon cross-racial sisterhood – that is, while
their concerns are related, womanists are critical of feminists.
In particular, womanists have been keen to identify the racist
strategies among feminists in Church, society and history.
Arguably the most important womanist work in this area

was Jacquelyn Grant's classic study of White and Black women during slavery.[8] Similarly, in the UK context, Hazel Carby produced a important analysis of the tensions between Black and White feminism in the early 1980s.[9]

Finally, womanist theologians engage in a quest for socio-political wholeness. Because their analysis is multifaceted, womanist theologians seek ways to ensure the liberty and well-being of all. This is why womanist theology is also a liberation theology.[10] Socio-political wholeness means freedom, justice and well-being for all in the community[11] – an approach which links Black women's struggles to other liberation movements in Black communities. Kelly Brown Douglas argues that the Civil Rights Movement is a paradigm of this process.[12] Similarly, Elaine Foster has identified these trends among Black women in the Church in Britain.[13] As well as being multidimensional, socio-political wholeness is also bifocal, covering issues of oppression inside and outside Black communities.[14] Bifocality suggests that issues of oppression within Black communities – such as the prevalence of Eurocentric images of beauty and lateral (Black-on-Black) violence – are as important as racist attacks and structural racism in employment and education. Contrary to the assertions of many Black British Pentecostalists that religion and politics do not mix, socio-political wholeness is not devoid of a transforming spirituality – indeed, the two are synonymous here. Hence, to be active in improving the welfare of marginalised Black women is to be a part of the redeeming work of Christ in the world.[15]

Womanist theology in Britain

Although of North American origins, womanist theology has influenced the lives of Black women in Britain. In Britain, womanist theology is in its embryonic stages. This does not mean, however, that Black women have avoided theological discourse: on the contrary, they have been conduits of Black theological concerns since Africans were brought from the shores of Africa to the Caribbean. However, due to the subjugation and marginalisation of Black women in Church and society, their voices have been muted.

Significantly, in recent Black British history, there have been two major attempts to use written texts to make known womanist perspectives on theology. A first generation emerged in the 1980s,[16] and a second in the mid 1990s.

The first group was primarily concerned with political activism and pastoral care. They sought to critique racism and sexism in the Church and their aim was the empowerment of Black women. For example, Elaine Foster, exploring issues inside the Black Church, writes of the 'inverted pyramid' which reflected the Church run by Black women, their ministries and spirituality. Foster, like Valentina Alexander, argues that Black women run the Church while men simply lead it. Furthermore, she argues that one way in which the Church can begin the process of ridding itself of sexism is by celebrating the achievements of Black women. This evocation of the historical memory of Black women in society and the Bible would provide a new framework for liberation. Such a language would not require Black women's having to seek or base their freedom on male interpretations of the Bible.[17] Another example from this generation of womanists is found in the reflections of

Eve Pitts. Commenting on Katie Canon's *Black Womanist Ethics* and writing from the perspective of a Black woman in a White Church, Pitts argues that Black women in Britain have much in common with their sisters in the USA. For example, Black women in Britain have created an ethical system which has enabled them to survive with integrity both the traumas of slavery and the terrors of life in racialised Britain.[18] This ethical system is based on the resources and perspectives gained by Black women in the course of their triple oppression – of race, class and gender. Despite the insights offered by these Black 'sisters', the perspectives they bring have generally been avoided by White feminists in both the academic world and the Church.[19] For example, an anthology of feminist theology, published in 1990, made no mention of Black women in Britain, or anywhere else in the world!

A second generation of British womanist theologians has emerged in the mid 1990s. While retaining the pastoral and activist concerns of the first generation, they have added a sharp, contextual, academic focus to their womanism. For example, Jill Brown[20] was drawn to womanist theology both because it took seriously the experiences of Black women, and because of its holistic concern for liberation for all marginalised groups. In her words: 'It allows me to validate my own experiences'. Christology is an important focus for Brown's womanism: she is concerned with asking questions about the contemporary relevance of Jesus Christ for Black women. While feminists are concerned about whether a male Saviour can save women, Brown argues that Black women see Jesus in very different terms – for example, his maleness is not as important as his humanity. Even so, Brown feels that issues of Jesus' suffering are still problematic – the concept of redemptive suffering has so often been used to oppress women in the Church. In other words, theology often makes Black women feel that their suffering is God-given. Brown is also concerned about finding new ways of articulating the theological concerns of Black women – ways which make Black women's language the central form of expression. She feels that there is too much jargon in theological circles which is not understood by, or even relevant to, Black communities. Hence, she is currently working with alternative, everyday Afrocentric spiritual traditions in the Black community in an attempt to find a new language to express what is special about Jesus for Black women today.

Whereas Brown is concerned with the meaning of Jesus today, Kate Coleman[21] is concerned with Black women in leadership. As the only Black Baptist woman minister in Britain, Coleman has drawn upon her life experience and personal circumstances to construct a womanist theology. She argues that a womanist theology within Britain must take seriously its quest to be holistic. Despite sexism being a major issue for Black women, she argues that both Black men and Black women still have to deal with the brutality of racism in British society. In a similar fashion, Novette Thompson[22] is exploring the relationship between womanist theology and pastoral care. Like Coleman, she seeks to use the experiences of Black women in order to construct a womanist approach which empowers Black people on the margins of both Church and society.

However, some within the new school of womanist theologians are making their starting-point outside the Black Church tradition. For example, Valentina Alexander's[23] womanist theology is informed less by traditional American womanist theology and more by a more personal quest to make sense of her experience as a Black British woman. Spirituality is a central aspect of this quest, and womanist theology but one of many ways of interpreting

her concerns. Alexander is particularly concerned about the
mythology of Black women being 'really together'. The
recent upsurge in Black male groups, Black male survival
literature and educational concerns about Black male
children has focused attention away from the issues and
concerns of Black women. While these concerns are
genuine, she is not convinced that they are as important as
the issues facing Black women. For example, in a recent
conversation on the educational needs of Black children,
she said:

> In schools, as well as the problems faced by Black
> boys, there are crucial issues concerning young Black
> women, such as self-esteem. If they are not dealt with,
> they can often result in destructive relationships and
> mental stagnation. It's too easy for Black women to
> learn to prioritise other people's needs above their
> own.[24]

Another womanist whose works draw on non-traditional
Christian sources is Michelle Campbell.[25] Campbell's
starting-point is development theory. She argues that womanists cannot avoid global inequality. Moreover, the
inequality faced by Black women in the West should resonate with many issues of global inequality. She contends
that Black Christians need to re-evaluate their mission in
the world. While she is aware of the long-standing traditions
of informal development among diasporan people who pour
resources into projects 'back home', she is critical of the
way in which many Black Christians in Britain have been
quick to adopt selfish prosperity doctrines at the expense of
development programmes in the Third World. She states:
'Instead of just being concerned with the building of
churches in the UK, Black Churches need to raise awareness

and get involved in changing the economic conditions in the Third World'. Campbell wants to place issues of gender in a wider global context of economic exploitation and political marginalisation. Furthermore, she believes that there are important lessons to be learned from the interaction between womanist theologies and models of global development. As with the first generation, the perspectives of this second generation of womanist theologians have generally gone unacknowledged in the wider, White feminist theological community, and also in the Black academic feminist community.[26]

What can we learn from womanism?

It is not my place, as a Black man, to construct womanist theology. My intention here is not to evaluate womanist theology as a theological system by examining Alice Walker's definition, or its application by womanists. Instead, it is befitting that we all learn from the contemporary consciousness of Black women in order to develop a holistic Christian spirituality and practice – a process which includes listening to the experiences of Black women. To this end, this chapter has been primarily concerned with giving recognition to the emerging womanist critique in the Church, through its advocates. As a Black male theologian, I am limited in terms of evaluating and getting inside the consciousness of Black women. Even so, part of the process of my own personal growth and development must be to interact with the developments that have taken place so far. Several issues emerge from this brief study.

First, the emergence of womanist theology in Britain

demands repentance and renewal from all Black men. We men cannot kid ourselves that we are not sexist, and therefore do not need to engage with the programme. Sexism is alive and well in many of our minds, hearts and Churches. By acknowledging this fact we can begin the process of renewal.

Second, renewal is related to what womanist theology has to say to Black men. It encourages a wholesale re-examination of both Church life and academic life. Black men in the Church and in academia must do more than pay lip-service to the presence and achievements of Black women: we must be transformed by a womanist consciousness. Such a conversion process involves not only becoming competent in the tools of womanist scholarship, but also, on another level, involves our 'hearing' Black women. Black people know all too well that hearing is not a passive activity; hearing means *doing*. That is why the Jamaican proverb relates hearing to the significance of doing, and the danger of passivity, when it says 'If you don't hear, you will feel' – that is, not hearing criticism will lead you to experience pain in the long run. Furthermore, hearing is a powerful means of bringing about change. That is why, in the New Testament, Paul informs us that faith comes by 'hearing'. Hearing Black women, in this sense, therefore means that we have to cultivate a radical solidarity and a productive empathy with them.

Third (and related to the second point), womanist theology encourages Black men to build a new partnership with women – a partnership which is not based on the old premises of Black patriarchy, but which makes the mutual quests for Black wholeness its core. This means that Black men must cultivate a spirit of openness and humility. Openness means being open to the needs of Black women, and also open to a new spirituality which will reconstruct Black maleness. Humility concerns putting to death the myths about male supremacy that we have passed on for generations. Cultivating openness and humility will not save us from our sexism – it is just the beginning: these qualities might enable us to get to the negotiating table alongside our sisters.

Finally, womanist theology encourages a healthy suspicion towards all movements, organisations and programmes within the Black community. Womanist perspectives encourage us to ask whose needs are being met and also whose agenda is being played out. In short, new developments – such as the rise of Islam, the emergence of British Afrocentrism, and African-centred religions – must all be scrutinised through womanist paradigms. For example, Black men choosing to adopt religious, cultural and philosophical concerns would be wise to mobilise a womanist critique.

In conclusion, Alice Walker's definition and description of 'womanist', quoted at the beginning of this chapter, has had profound effect upon Black theological communities in Britain. British womanist theology, while in its embryonic stages, has taken a lead from African–American women in order to explore and outline a new theology which prioritises Black women. The work of the second and third generation of womanists in Britain has much to say to Black men in the Church and society. It bespeaks a new relationship between Black men and women based on sound ideas and meaningful practices.

9 Forgive and forget? a Black Christian political rereading of the Lord's Prayer

One of the most dynamic aspects of the Pentecostal Church tradition is the prayer meeting. Prayer within the Pentecostal Church is corporate: we all pray together. There is something unifying as well as invigorating about praying in the presence of God, along with your brothers and sisters in Christ. That's why Pentecostalists love the verse which says that where two or three are gathered in God's name, God is in the midst of them. This text is a mandate for our corporacy.

Another aspect of prayer within the Pentecostal Church tradition is the form of prayer. To pray in this tradition is to create an intricate interweaving of song, Scripture and folk-saying with personal or corporate need. Whether spoken softly or expressed in ecstatic exclamation, these ingredients are held together by the deep existential longings of people who know what it means to be on the outside looking in. This kind of prayer, at its best, is not just spiritual petitioning but also an art form.[1]

Prayer and the reader's response to Scripture

As a Black theologian, I find that the most interesting aspect of Pentecostal prayer is the way in which we reread Scripture. We reread Scripture as a result of our interaction with the text – an interaction which is a natural product of the African–Caribbean tradition of 'call and response'. This form of dialogue between a speaker and congregation has its origins in traditional African societies. The tradition of 'call and response' ensures that we always respond to the reading of Scripture at prayer meetings, especially when we are conscious that the word of God is feeding us anew. There are various levels of response to the reading of Scripture. First, there are liturgical responses which are used to acknowledge the end or beginning of the reading. These responses affirm the importance of God's word, particularly its power to reach us, transform us and speak into our existence. A second level of response to Scripture reading – and the one which is of most importance to me – is the reaction to particular concepts or themes within the text. If the Scripture reading moves us, then we say 'Amen'. If the text really registered, then we say 'Hallelujah'. Hermeneut-ically speaking, these responses are oral affirmations which recompose the meaning of the text to fit with the needs of our contemporary situation. This 'meeting of two horizons' – that of the text and that of the lives of Black people in church – produces a rereading: new meanings arise as we affirm a passage, theme or concept. This is what Hans Jauss calls 'horizons of expectation': the meaning of texts fitting in a particular historical moment.[2]

On reflection, it was during these 'sweet hours of prayer' that I was first introduced to a form of reader-response criticism. Reader-response criticism is not a uniform dis-cipline: it consists of various schools of thought which advocate various processes and techniques.[3] Put simply, reader-response relocates the *meaning* of a biblical passage or text to the reader's own situation. Therefore, in order to discover its meaning for him or her, the reader explores the text in relation to his or her own context. Meaning is therefore found beyond the Bible, in the concrete world in which we live – rather than existing exclusively in the mind of the 'original' author, or in the historical background, shape or structure of the text. At its best, reader-response gives hermeneutical power to ordinary readers like the Black folk who taught me to understand the Bible at Sunday school. At its worst, reader-response can legitimise oppressive readings of the text. This is often the consequence of neglecting two things – first, the influence of community, and second, the valuable historicity of texts. Such neglect produces the likes of David Koresh.

The version of reader-response which I learned at prayer meetings was always communal. Together, we worked out, struggled through or stumbled upon the meaning of a passage. The responses of verbal affirmation or complete silence were a clue to those 'interpreting' that their thoughts were acceptable or errant. Consequently, our rereadings were subject to prescribed reading conventions – that is, the doctrinal affiliations of our Church. As well as being communal, our reader-response was also spiritual. We believed that the Holy Spirit was guiding us in the process of applying God's word. Consequently, I found that when 'in the Spirit', I best understood how to apply Scripture. 'Pneumatic hermeneutics' is how one scholar describes this process.[4]

Our reader-response was also dialogical. The emphasis was not exclusively upon the reader or the text: instead, we inhabited a middle ground, where we would wrestle with the meaning of Scripture. This Scripture–context dialectic began with believers praying for the Spirit of God to lead them into a new understanding of a particular passage of Scripture. Often that new understanding arose from a life-encounter, which then brought about a new evaluation of the passage.

Another feature of prayer-meeting hermeneutics was that our reading was intimately related to action. Reading the Bible was geared towards our becoming better Christian people. Therefore, new understandings of the Bible were supposed to propel us into a new praxis. Reading was not just about what went on in our heads, but was also deeply connected to transforming our lives. The text was pharma-cosmic – it had the power to heal.[5]

Finally, our rereading was limited by our theology. For example, when I was a member of the Wesleyan Holiness Church, we were indoctrinated to transcend issues of race, class or gender oppression. Consequently, these issues were not fully brought to bear upon the text. This does not mean that we did not find ways of raising these issues and requesting deliverance – but our socio-political concerns were mostly hidden beneath coded requests for God's power in prayers which spoke of 'keeping on', 'troubles at work', or 'evil in the world'. Even so, our general denial of these issues meant that we remained imprisoned by reading conventions which limited what we could say was in the Bible.

This last point has become an important issue for me, as I have learned more about theology, and simultaneously have had my reading conventions broadened and challenged. For example, engagement with Black theology in America and the Caribbean has made me more aware of how Black and womanist theologians bring the holistic concerns of the Black community to their reading of the Bible. Such a process includes awareness of social and political issues, a concern for justice and an unyielding desire for action.[6] As a consequence, when I read the Bible today, I read it anew from a Black Christian political perspective. On the one hand, this perspective for rereading is beset by limitations:

being a Black heterosexual man, of liberal Black Pentecostal persuasion, with a particular formal and informal educational background, I am limited in the way in which I reread. On the other hand, this perspective on rereading, while acknowledging its limitations, still has the potential to be liberating: a powerful, uplifting experience which brings God's revelation in the Bible to bear on my existence in order that I might experience God's liberating activity in my life. This kind of rereading is Dread.[7] For marginalised people, the limitations of reader-response rarely outweigh the benefits. So what happens when I read from this perspective?

I have chosen to demonstrate this particular reading convention by exploring Matthew 6:1–15. Significantly, this text concerns prayer, as I want to critique the process of prayer that undergirds the prayer meetings which I continue to attend as a Black Christian in a Black-led church.

'Take care! Don't do your good deeds publicly, to be admired, for then you will lose the reward from your Father in heaven. When you give a gift to a beggar, don't shout about it as the hypocrites do – blowing trumpets in the synagogues and streets to call attention to their acts of charity! I tell you in all earnestness, they have received all the reward they will ever get. But when you do a kindness to someone do it secretly – don't tell your left hand what your right hand is doing. And your Father who knows all secrets will reward you. And now about prayer. When you pray, don't be like the hypocrites who pretend piety by praying publicly on street corners and in the synagogues where everyone can see them. Truly, that is all the reward they will ever get. But when you pray, go away by yourself, all alone, and shut the door behind you

and pray to our Father secretly, and your Father, who knows your secrets, will reward you. Don't recite the same prayer over and over as the heathen do, who think prayers are answered only by repeating them again and again. Remember, your Father knows exactly what you need even before you ask him! Pray along these lines: Our Father in heaven, we honour your holy name. We ask that your kingdom will come now. May your will be done here on earth, just as it is in heaven. Give us our food again today, as usual, and forgive us our sins, just as we have forgiven those who have sinned against us. Don't bring us into temptation, but deliver us from the Evil One. Amen.'
(Matt. 6:1–15, The Living Bible)

Two themes emerge from this passage when it is reread from a Black Christian political perspective. They are *subversive piety* and *prophetic petitioning*.

Subversive piety

Jesus contrasts subversive piety with popularist spirituality. Subversive piety is a radical devotion to God, which is not always obvious, but which is geared towards social change. That's why Jesus encourages people to give alms in secret. This is an important strategy, not only because it nurtures a spirit of humility, but also because it enables liberation activity to take place away from those who would want to restrain it. In contrast, a popularist spirituality is an artificial holiness based on show, with no substance – and is therefore an affirmation of the *status quo*. This form of godliness lacks real, liberating power.

A subversive piety has been manifest throughout African–
Caribbean history, in both secular and spiritual forms. For
example, during slavery in Jamaica, the secular form produced the Quarshie. The Quarshie was the docile image
which slaves used in order to mask their revolutionary aspirations.[8] To a certain degree, the Quarshie was the
personification of Anancy the spider. Anancy stories were
folk-tales from Africa fecund with wise sayings and doings.
In short, Anancy always 'acted the fool in order to catch
the wise'.

During slavery, the Christian version of subversive piety
was found among the Christian people involved in slave
rebellions. One only has to read the accounts of slave revolts
in the Caribbean to notice the cunning, guile and deception
used by Christian leaders – particularly in Sam Sharpe's
rebellion in 1831–2, in Jamaica. Sharpe, a 'freed' Baptist
minister, used his status and relative freedom as a slave
preacher to nurture a subversive piety among his congregations. Essentially, he encouraged the slaves not to practise
publicly their God-inspired radical devotion geared towards
social change (that is, freedom) until the time was right.
Sharpe used the relative privacy of slave prayer meetings to
plan insurrection. This presents an important paradigm for
the Black Church at prayer – of the prayer meeting as a
sacred space for mobilisation against the forces of injustice.
Such was Sharpe's effectiveness that within a year he had
organised the most successful rebellion in Jamaican history.

Unfortunately, subversive piety appears to have died out
in African–Caribbean Christianity after slavery. African–
Caribbean Christianity preferred the security of popularist
spirituality.[9] By the twentieth century, subversive piety had
found a more suitable home in the early attempts to develop
liberation theology in the Caribbean, in Garveyism and later
in Rastafari.[10] This development was a tragedy for Jamaican

Christianity; today it still seeks to rid itself of socio-political passivity.[11]

Subversive piety is a dangerous commodity which needs to be a part of the spirituality of any Church which is seriously concerned with holistic renewal. However, in Britain today, subversive piety has not totally deserted the Black Church: many display a weak subversive piety, in which this radical devotion to God is softened, being geared towards *limited* social change. As Valentina Alexander has pointed out, this weak manifestation can be seen in the tradition of passive radicalism.[12]

Prophetic petitioning

The second issue which emerges when I reread this passage in Matthew's Gospel is prophetic petitioning.

> Pray along these lines: Our Father in heaven, we honour your holy name. We ask that your kingdom will come now. May your will be done here on earth, just as it is in heaven. Give us our food again today, as usual, and forgive us our sins, just as we have forgiven those who have sinned against us. Don't bring us into temptation, but deliver us from the Evil One.

Much can be said about the petitions, all of which is of great significance when the text is read from this perspective.

Intimacy

First, we can comment on the use of the words 'Our Father'. Emerging womanist theologians in Britain adopt a critical approach to the text which rethinks the masculine imagery used of God.[13] Although many Black Churches still insist upon viewing God as male, womanists encourage us to look afresh at the use of the word 'Father'. In this case, it is clear that 'Father' is not a literal description of God's maleness, but rather a plea for an intimate relationship.

Intimacy is one area of Pentecostal theology that you just can't fake: you know when you're close to God. Even so, spiritual hype is always a danger within Black Churches. Spiritual hype is when loudness, sensationalism and physical or emotional ecstasy take precedence over a genuine connection with, and sensitivity to, the moving of God's Spirit. This does not mean that God is not present in the expressive physicality[14] of Black worship, but that expressive physicality cannot be a substitute for intimacy with God. I know that I have often fallen into this trap. For instance, I remember once being on a panel to discuss church-based projects in the community. The meeting was being held at a branch of the Church of God of Prophecy, so before we started the meeting officially, we had some serious communal prayer. I began praying, with the usual things I say in order to focus on God. But as I continued, I could hear a man at the back of the room praying with great depth and such intimacy – he even ended his prayer by saying, 'I got to go now, Lord'. His prayer epitomised the kind of intimacy that Jesus was talking about. In comparison, my prayer seemed superficial.

A God of action

Reading from a Black Christian political perspective, the words, 'we hallow your holy name' are also significant. At this point, Jewish traditions of reverence join with the reverencing of African religions.[15] Here, giving God a hallowed status also means that we expect God to act as a consequence of his holiness. 'Hallowed is your name' is therefore a request for action. In the Black Church tradition there is a strong belief in the notion of a God of action – however, the locus of God's activity is often reduced to the 'spiritual realm'. This means that God's activity, while primarily supernatural, occurs in the personal, individual lives of human beings. This is why Black Christians have so many songs about God being active in their physical lives, for example:

> God is not dead, he is still alive
> God is not dead, he is still alive
> I can feel him in my hands
> I can feel him in my feet
> I can feel him all over
> Feel him all over me.

While this chorus affirms the individual as a temple of the Holy Spirit, and politically affirms divine presence among Black folk, it also highlights a problem in the Black Church. The problem here is the unwillingness to acknowledge openly and categorically the importance of the work of God in the world, especially in social structures and by means of people as agents of change. The closest that Black church songs get to acknowledging God's presence outside the Church is when they are about the missionary work of the Spirit:

> All over the world
> The Spirit is moving
> All over the world
> As the prophet said it would be.

This unwillingness to see God in systems, structures and institutions limits our potential for a holistic theology, in which God's redeeming work is truly omnipresent in Black communities. Consequently, Black churches often fail to direct their spiritual energy towards the specific social and political needs within their communities.

Kingdom come!

Another significant part of my rereading of the Lord's Prayer is the prophetic petition: 'We ask that your kingdom will come now. May your will be done here on earth, just as it is in heaven.' This is serious stuff. It's one thing to ask, 'Can I have a good day, Lord?', but quite another to request, 'Let your Kingdom come' – that is a big one! For some scholars, the coming of the Kingdom is partially realised in the following petitions: 'Give us our food again today, as usual, forgive our sins just as we have forgiven those who have sinned against us. Don't bring us into temptation, but deliver us from the Evil One. Amen.'

Reading this from my perspective, daily bread is significant. Black Pentecostalists have a strong, unwavering belief that God will 'supply all of our needs', according to God's riches in glory. This belief is played out at 'testimony time', when believers provide psychological and material evidence of God's providence. Even when people experience tragedy in their lives, they still search for God's providence. At its best, this approach to tragedy and despair produces a profound theology of hope, born from adversity and resistance. But at its worst, it gives life to a shallow theology of hope which leads to a false understanding of the human condition, and fosters an avoidance of wrestling with pain and suffering. This is akin to having the resurrection without the crucifixion. For example, I remember going to the funeral of a young child in my congregation, at which no attempt was made to focus on the tragic loss; instead, the service focused exclusively on praise and thanksgiving for the life that had been lived. Such imbalance fails to search for the meaning of providence in the chaotic world in which we live.

The reality of evil

Deliverance from evil is also an important theme in my rereading of the text. The syncretism of Christianity with West African cosmologies has led to the development of an African–Caribbean British Christianity which takes seriously the presence of evil in the cosmos. Black churches in Britain must be some of the few places where people talk openly about the Devil and the persistence of evil. I know that in trendy theological colleges, such talk is often viewed as pathological or pre-scientific. Many explanations of the workings of evil which are given in Black churches may indeed fall into such categories – but the general unwillingness to talk about evil in White theological circles reflects a problematic theodicy. The idea of 'fate' often supplants evil in an analysis of society – and as a result, the forces of evil are reduced to, and explained as, 'the consequences of modern life'. The result of this perception is that the forces of evil go unchecked. For example, I once suggested that staff should meet together for special prayer and fasting in order to confront a particular crisis in college. I had sensed that we were not just 'wrestling with flesh and blood', and that the matter required serious petitioning to God, and warfare against supernatural forces which were working against us. There was a negative response to my Black Pentecostal analysis; instead, 'consequential' explanations won the day.

Forgiveness and oppression

From my perspective, the petition, 'Forgive our sins just as we have forgiven those who have sinned against us', is deeply problematical. At this point another tradition of the Black Church comes into effect. Black Christianity has often challenged given or traditional interpretations so as to 'read against' the biblical text, and relied upon alternative sources for evaluating the will of God. That's why the injunction, 'Slaves, obey your masters', was never taken seriously by Black slaves on Caribbean plantations.[16] Likewise, reading against the text provided the theological motivation for the refusal of abolitionists like Sojourner Truth to believe that women were inferior to men. So when I read this section, on the one hand, I take seriously the importance of forgiveness – that is, one can't be Christian without forgiveness. But on the other hand, because of Black people's continuing history of marginalisation, I add the proviso: 'So long as the oppression continues, we can forgive but we can't afford to forget'. In other words, when I pray this prayer, I mean: 'Forgive us our sins as we forgive those who sin against us, but let us not forget, while the oppression and coercion continue'.

This is not a unique approach to forgiveness. For example, when I was in South Africa, I discovered that, while Black Christians had forgiven their White oppressors, they were not ready to forget, for fear of becoming complacent about injustice. This stance was not a form of malicious vindictiveness. Like those involved in the Reparations Movement in Britain, the Black Christians in South Africa maintained their common memory for the sake of ensuring the wholeness of humanity in the present and future. To a degree, this is what God encouraged Israel to do by remembering 'that they were once slaves in Egypt'. In this Old Testament example, maintaining past memories was an essential aspect of upholding present justice and offering thanksgiving. This is not as one-sided as it may initially seem: if the historical memory ensures vigilance among the victimised, it may prevent and transform the present acts of the perpetrators. In such cases the freedom of the perpetrators is safeguarded by the actions of the victimised – as Fanon has shown, historical memory can prevent new acts of brutality against, or by, the oppressed.[17] However, this is not always a foolproof process – the ways in which oppressed people have become oppressors tell us that justice cannot totally depend on the mobilisation of historical memory. In sum, though, this rereading of forgiveness is itself liberating.

Centred on Christ

In conclusion, I must mention another aspect of the prayer meeting within the Black Church: its Christocentric focus – that is, the way in which Christ becomes the mediator of our prayers and the broker of all our concerns. The prayer

meeting makes it clear that we can get nowhere without
Jesus. So no matter how we reread the text, we are always
brought in check by the stories about Jesus in the Bible.
The themes of the cross and the resurrection cause our
rereading to be guided by the redeeming work of Christ.
So what, then, does this focus mean in this particular
rereading of the Lord's Prayer? There are two concluding
remarks. First, Christocentricity means that rereadings must
be validated by the Church, which is the Body of Christ,
and cannot be read in isolation. As I stated above, commu-
nality is a fundamental dimension of both prayer and
hermeneutics in the Black Church. Second, it means that
Christ must be central to our struggle to interpret the text.
This will ensure that our rereadings will bespeak a socio-
political wholeness[18] that brings the liberating Gospel of
Christ to bear on every aspect of human life.

References

Introduction

1. See Stuart Hall, 'Cultural identity and diaspora', in Jonathan Rutherford, *Identity, Community Culture, Difference*, (London, Lawrence and Wishart, 1990).
2. Audre Lorde, *Sister Outsider* (California, The Crossing Press, 1984).
3. See Ronald Nathan, *The Voice* (20 May 1996).
4. First, the acknowledgement of one Supreme Being who is creator and sustainer of all (for example, *Olundumare* among the Yoruba). The Supreme Being is not always presented as father-figure (God as male): in matriarchal societies the Supreme Being was a mother-figure, as is the case among the Nuba in Kenya. Second, in ancient African religious traditions, because God is understood as being both immanent and transcendent (near and far), Africans viewed themselves as being able to interact daily with the spiritual world. Within this framework of expression, super-rational experiences such as dreams, visions and miraculous occurrences were legitimate forms of divine–human communication. Third, another theme in traditional African religion is the veneration of the ancestors. Ancestor veneration occurs for a variety of reasons, including maintaining lineage and because they are models of good lifestyle. Also, African traditional religions emphasise a balance between the individual and the group. John Mbiti's statement, 'I am because we are, and since we are, therefore I am', sums up this relationship. Finally, traditional African religions stressed a concept of the afterlife. Death was another stage in life where one took on the form of an ancestor or spirit. See John Mbiti, *African Religions and Philosophy* (Garden City, NY, Anchor Books, 1970).
5. Edward Kamau Braithwaite, *Folk Culture of the Slaves in Jamaica* (London, New Beacon Books, 1970), p. 6.
6. Albert J. Raboteau, *Slave Religion: The Invisible Institution in the Antebellum South* (Oxford, Oxford University Press, 1978), pp. 4–5.
7. Iain Macrobert, 'The Black roots of Pentecostalism', in Jan A. B.

Jongeneel, *et al.* (eds), *Pentecost, Mission and Ecumenism, Essays on Intercultural Theology* (Frankfurt, Peter Lang, 1992), p. 76.

8. Iain Macrobert, 'The Black roots of Pentecostalism'.

9. See Walter Hollenweger, *The Pentecostals* (London, SCM Press, 1972); and Iain Macrobert, *Black Roots and White Racism in Early Pentecostalism in the USA* (London, Macmillan Press, 1988).

10. See Roswith Gerloff, *A Plea for Black British Theologies, The Black Church Movement in Britain in its Trans-Atlantic Cultural and Theological Interaction,* (Frankfurt, Peter Lang, 1992), Vol. 1.

11. Iain Macrobert, *Black Roots and White Racism,* p. 80.

12. For a more systematic account, see Iain Macrobert, *Black Pentecostalism – its Origins, Functions and Theology* Unpublished PhD Thesis, (University of Birmingham, 1989).

13. See Winston James and Clive Harris (eds), *Inside Babylon: The Caribbean Diaspora in Britain* (England, Verso, 1993).

14. See Leon Murray, *Being Black in Britain: Challenge and Hope* (London, Clifford Frost Ltd, 1995), pp. 11ff.

15. See Harvey Cox, *Fire From Heaven: The Rise of Pentecostal Spirituality and the Reshaping of Religion in the Twenty-First Century* (London, Cassell, 1996).

16. For a summary, see the introduction in James Cone and Gayraud Wilmore (eds), *Black Theology: a Documentary History,* Vol. 2. 1980–1992 (Maryknoll, NY, Orbis, 1992).

17. See Paul Gilroy, *The Black Atlantic, Modernity and Double Consciousness* (London, Verso, 1993).

18. Raymond Williams, *Culture* (Glasgow, Fontana, 1981), p. 13.

19. See Iain Chambers, *Boarder Dialogue* (New York, Routledge, 1990).

20. See Paul Gilroy, 'One nation under a groove: the cultural politics of "race" and racism in Britain', in David Theo Goldberg (ed.), *Anatomy of Racism* (Minneapolis, University of Minnesota Press, 1990).

21. 'Racialised' is used throughout to mean the way in which the concept of race is conferred on a group within a given context. 'Racial' is the process of using racist concepts.

Chapter 1 Independent intravenshan by the rivers of Babylon: the Black Church and resistance

1. Elaine Foster, 'The inverted pyramid', in Gita Sahgal and Nira Yuval-Davis (eds), *Refusing Holy Orders* (London, Virago Press, 1992).
2. ibid.
3. See Valentina Alexander, 'A mouse in a jungle: the Black Christian woman's experience in the church and society in Britain', in Delia Jarrett-Macauley (ed.), *Reconstructing Womanhood, Reconstructing Feminism, Writings on Black Women* (London, Routledge, 1996), pp. 85–109.
4. *The Voice* (24 March 1997), p. 27.
5. Cornel West, *Prophetic Fragments* (Grand Rapids, Eerdmans, 1988).
6. See Cornel West, *Race Matters* (Boston, Beacon Press, 1994).
7. Simon Horne, 'Making the body whole', in Frances Young (ed.) *Encounter with Mystery* (London, DLT, 1997).
8. ibid.
9. See Winston James and Clive Harris (eds), *Inside Babylon: The Caribbean Diaspora in Britain* (England, Verso, 1993).
10. James Cone, *For My People: Black Theology and the Black Church* (Maryknoll, NY, Orbis, 1984).
11. See Les Back, *New Ethnicities and Urban Culture* (London, UCL Press, 1996).
12. See Rosino Gabellini (ed.), *Paths of African Theology* (London, SCM Press, 1994).
13. Dwight Hopkins, *Black Theology, USA and South Africa* (Maryknoll, NY, Orbis, 1990).
14. Dr Randall Bailey.
15. These issues emerge from informal discussion with Dr Randall Bailey.
16. Octavius A. Gaba, 'Symbols of revelation: the darkness of the Hebrew Yahweh and the light of the Greek Logos', in Randall C. Bailey and Jacquelyn Grant (eds), *The Recovery of Black Presence, An Interdisciplinary Exploration* (Nashville, Abingdon Press, 1995), pp. 143–59.
17. See Paul Gilroy, *There Ain't No Black in the Union Jack* (London, Unwin Hyman, 1987).
18. Valentina Alexander, *Breaks Every Fetter? To What Extent has the*

Black-led Church in Britain Developed a Theology of Liberation? Unpublished PhD thesis (University of Warwick, 1996).

Chapter 2   What kind of freed slaves worship in the slavemaster's Church? Black resistance in White Churches in Britain

1. A. Sivanandan, 'From resistance to rebellion: Asian and Afro-Caribbean struggles in Britain', *Race and Class* Vol. 23, 2–3 (Autumn 1981/Winter 1983), pp. 111–52.

2. There have been no Black students from the United Reformed Church at Queen's during my time there.

3. Stella Dazie, 'Searching for the invisible women: slavery and resistance in Jamaica' in *Race and Class*, Vol. 32, No. 2, (October–December, 1990), pp. 21–39.

4. See Kenneth Leech, *Struggle in Babylon, Racism in the Cities and Churches of Britain* (London, SPCK, 1988); John Wilkinson, *The Church in Black and White* (Edinburgh, St Andrew's Press, 1993); John Vincent and Chris Rowland, *Liberation Theology UK* (Sheffield, Urban Theology Unit, 1995).

5. The General Synod of the Church of England, *Seeds of Hope, Report of a Survey on Combating Racism in the Dioceses of the Church of England* (London, The General Synod of the Church of England, 1991).

6. Robinson Milwood, *Liberating Mission, A Black Experience* (London, African Resource Centre, 1997).

7. The General Synod of the Church of England, *The Passing Winter* (London, The General Synod of the Church of England, 1997).

8. *Liberation Mission*, p. 89

9. ibid.

10. ibid., p.xiv

11. ibid., pp. 96–7

12. ibid., p. 11

13. ibid., p. 15

14. ibid., pp. 24, 96

15. ibid., p. 101

16. *The Passing Winter*, p. 24.

17. ibid., p. 36

18. ibid., p. 30
19. ibid., p. 10
20. ibid., p. 43
21. *Church Times* (13 June 1997), p. 5.
22. *The Passing Winter*, p. 40.
23. bell hooks, *Black Looks*, Race and Representation (London, Turnaround, 1992).
24. Martin Luther King, *Strength to Love* (Philadelphia, Fortress Press, 1981), pp. 9ff.
25. See Richard Hart, *Slaves who Abolished Slavery* (2 vols) (Jamaica, Insitute of Social and Economic Research, 1980).
26. J. L. Segundo, *The Liberation of Theology* (NY, Orbis, 1972).
27. bell hooks and Cornel West, *Breaking Bread, Insurgent Black Intellectual Life* (Boston MA, South End Press, 1991).
28. op. cit.

Chapter 3   The Masai have a point: Black male sexual representation and Christology

1. As we shall see later, because these representations transcend the influence and control of the state, it is necessary to explore alternative responses outside the realms of traditional political struggle.
2. Toinette M. Eugene, 'While love is unfashionable: ethical implications of Black spirituality and sexuality', in James Nelson and Sandra Longfellow (eds), *Sexuality and the Sacred: Sources for Theological Reflection*, London, Mowbray, 1994), pp. 105–14.
3. Henry Louis Gates, Jr, 'The Black man's burden', in Gina Dent (ed.), *Black Popular Culture* (Seattle, Bay Press, 1992).
4. Stuart Hall, 'Cultural identity and diaspora,' in bell hooks, *Black Looks: Race and Representation* (London, Turnaround Press, 1992), p. 3.
5. Stuart Hall, 'Cultural identity and cinematic representation', *Framework*, pp. 36, 70.
6. Robert E. Hood, *Begrimed and Black: Christian Traditions on Blacks and Blackness* (USA, Augsburg Fortress, 1994), pp. 24–43.
7. According to Joseph Washington, Christian symbolism – its equation of good and evil with light and dark, along with the tendency of

conquered peoples to demonise their foes – led to medieval European art representing Black bodies as grotesque and prone to evil. These representations inform us about White fears of Black sexuality. According to Washington, these fears are represented in Shakespeare's depiction of 'Blackamoors'. See Joseph Washington, *Anti-Blackness in English Religion, 1500–1900*, (Lewiston, NY, Edwin Mellen Press, 1984).

8. Robert Miles, *Racism* (London, Routledge, 1984), Chapter 1.
9. Peter Fryer is keen to show that not all early representations were negative. See Peter Fryer, *Staying Power: the History of Black People in Britain* (London, Pluto Press, 1984), Chapter 4.
10. ibid., pp. 140, 159.
11. ibid., pp. 135–90.
12. Peter Fryer, *Staying Power*, pp. 165 ff.
13. Robert Miles, *Racism*, p. 33.
14. Homi K. Bhabha, 'The other question: the stereotype and colonial discourse', in *Screen*, 24, 4 (1983), 18.
15. Steven Small, *Racialised Barriers: The Black Experience in the United States and England in the 1980s* (London, Routledge, 1994), p. 97.
16. Steven Small, *Racialised Barriers*, p. 99.
17. *Cracker* was screened in the winter of 1994.
18. ibid.
19. A good study on the presentation of Black people in the media is found in bell hooks, *Black Looks*.
20. Patricia Hill Collins, *Black Feminist Thought: Knowledge, Consciousness and the Politics of Empowerment* (New York & London, Routledge, 1991).
21. Robert Staples, *Black Masculinity: The Black Man's Role in American Society* (San Francisco, Black Scholars Press, 1982).
22. Collins has identified how controlling images of Black women constructed during slavery (the Mammy, Matriarch, Jezebel and Breeder Woman) are reworked today in order to ensure that the blame for structural sources of poverty are shifted away from the state on to the Black women. Similarly, Robert Staples argues that images of Black men from the lazy Negro to the dangerous Black stud were constructed in a slave context in order to control the masculinity of Black men.
23. Frantz Fanon, *Black Skins, White Masks* (London, Pluto Press, 1993).
24. Patricia Hill Collins, *Black Feminist Thought*, p. 708.

25. ibid.

26. ibid., pp. 206 ff.

27. ibid.

28. I include myself because I do not believe that it is necessary to claim objectivity in this form of discourse.

29. Patricia Hill Collins, *Black Feminist Thought*, pp. 82 ff.

30. bell hooks, *Outlaw Culture: Resisting Representations* (New York & London, Routledge, 1994), pp. 115–23.

31. In response Black British gay filmmaker, Isaac Julien, in his films, *Looking for Langston* and *Young Soul Rebels*, has challenged the essentialising of Black male sexuality by portraying leading Black men in his films as both Black and gay, transgressing racial and sexual taboos in order to challenge the Black male policing of Black male sexuality. See, Isaac Julien, 'Black is, Black ain't: notes on de-essentializing Black identities', in Gina Dent (ed.), *Black Popular Culture* (Seattle, Bay Press, 1992) pp. 255–63.

32. See for example, James Nelson and Sandra Longfellow (eds), *Sexuality and the Sacred* (Westminster, John Knox Press, 1994).

33. Leo Steinberg, *The Sexuality of Christ in Renaissance Art and in Modern Oblivion* (New York, Pantheon Books, 1983).

34. Audre Lorde, *Sister Outsider* (California, The Crossing Press, 1984), pp. 53–9.

35. See Ira V. Brooks, *Another Gentleman to the Ministry* (Birmingham, Compeer Press, 1988).

36. I refer particularly to the work of Albert Cleague, James Cone, Malcolm X, Jacquelyn Grant and Kelly Douglas. See, Kelly Douglas, *The Black Christ* (Maryknoll, Orbis, 1994).

37. James Cone, *A Black Theology of Liberation* (Maryknoll, New York, 1987), pp. 119ff.

38. Jacquelyn Grant, *White Women's Christ and Black Women's Jesus, Feminist Christology and Womanist Response* (Atlanta, Scholars Press, 1988), p. 217.

39. Randall C. Bailey and Jacquelyn Grant (eds), *The Recovery of Black Presence, An Interdisciplinary Exploration* (Nashville, Abingdon Press, 1995), pp. 129–42.

40. Jacquelyn Grant, *White Woman's Christ, Black Woman's Jesus*; Grant talks about moving beyond Jesus' maleness to his humanity.

41. Audre Lorde, *Sister Outsider, Essays and Speeches* (California, The Crossing Press Feminist Series, 1994), pp. 40–45.

42. James Cone and Gayraud Wilmore (eds), *Black Theology, a Documentary History*, Vol. 2, 1980–1992 (Maryknoll, NY, Orbis, 1992).

Chapter 4   Art and Soul: Black Muslim art and Black theology

1. See J. S. Croatto, *Biblical Hermeneutics* (London, Orbis, 1989), p. x.
2. I refer here to the older generation of Black British who were known as West Indians.
3. See Ra Un Nefer Amen, *Metu Neter* (Brooklyn, NY, Khamit, 1990).
4. See The Womanist Theology Group, 'A womanist bibliodrama', in Raj Patel and Paul Grant (eds), *A Time to Act* (Nottingham, Russell Press, 1992), pp. 25–33.

Chapter 5   Watching you watching me: Black Christians in popular culture

1. *The Guardian* (3 January 1997).
2. See Chapter 7.
3. See John Vincent and Chris Rowland, *Liberation Theology UK* (Sheffield, Urban Theology Unit, 1995), pp. 17, 25.

Chapter 6   Jah would never give power to a Baldhead: Bob Marley as a Black liberation theologian

1. Paul Tillich, *Systematic Theology*, (Chicago, Chicago University Press, 1967), p. 3.
2. Carolyn Cooper, *Noises in the Blood: Gender, Orality and the Vulgar Body of Jamaican Popular Culture* (Durham, Duke University Press, 1995).
3. I have had numerous discussions with Black students who have told of their biblical studies lecturers' attitudes to Black and liberationist approaches to the text.

4. Bob Marley and the Wailers, *Time Will Tell*, *Kaya* (Island Records, 1978).
5. See Michio Ogata (ed.), *Rasta/Patois Dictionary*, updated 1995 (African Studies Web Site, 1996).
6. See *True Magazine* (May 1996).

Chapter 7   Jesus is Dread: language and Christology

1. See Ron Nathan, 'Issues for the Black minister', in Paul Grant and Raj Patel (eds), *A Time to Speak, Perspectives of Black Christians in Britain* (Nottingham, Russell Press, 1990), pp. 11–15.
2. See Ron Ramdin, *The Making of the Black Working Class in Britain* (England, Gower Publishing Company Limited, 1987), pp. 475–508.
3. Valentina Alexander, *Breaks Every Fetter. To What Extent has the Black-led Church in Britain Developed a Theology of Liberation?* Unpublished PhD thesis (Warwick University, 1996).
4. Roswith Gerloff, *A Plea for British Black Theologies, The Black Church Movement in Britain in its Transatlantic Cultural and Theological Interaction*, Vol.1 (Frankfurt, Peter Lang, 1992), p. 204.
5. See Gayraud Wilmore, 'Survival and liberation in Black faith', in Simon Maimela and Dwight Hopkins (eds), *We Are One Voice: Black Theology in the USA and South Africa* (Braamfontein, South Africa, Skotaville Publishers, 1989), pp. 1–33.
6. See Horace Campbell, *Rasta and Resistance, From Marcus Garvey to Walter Rodney* (London, Hansib Publications, 1985).
7. Stuart Hall, 'What is the Black in Black popular culture', in Gina Dent (ed.), *Black Popular Culture* (Seattle, Bay Press, 1992), p. 27.
8. See Paul Gilroy, *There Ain't No Black in the Union Jack* (Great Britain, Unwin Hyman, 1987), pp. 153–222.
9. Theo Smith, *Conjuring Culture, Biblical Formations of Black America* (New York and Oxford, Oxford University Press, 1994), p. 5–6.
10. James Cone, *A Black Theology of Liberation* (Second edition, Maryknoll, New York, Orbis Books, 1987), p. 27.
11. Roswith Gerloff, *A Plea for Black British Theologies, The Black Church Movement in Britain in its Transatlantic Cultural and Theological Interaction*, Vol. 1, pp. 221–6.
12. See Roger Hewitt, *White Talk Black Talk: Interracial Friendship and*

Communication Amongst Adolescents (Cambridge, Cambridge University Press, 1986).

13. Kobena Mercer, *Welcome to the Jungle, New Positions in Black Cultural Studies* (New York & London, Routledge, 1994), pp. 4–5.

14. See Steel Pulse, *Handsworth Revolution* (Island Records, 1978).

15. Aswad, *Live and Direct* (Island Records, 1981).

16. Robert E. Hood, *Must God Remain Greek, Afro Cultures and God-Talk* (Minneapolis, Fortress Press, 1992), pp. 63–4.

17. Victor Anderson, *Beyond Ontological Blackness* (New York, Continuum, 1995), p. 1.

18. Cornel West, *Race Matters* (New York, Beacon Press, 1994), pp. 1–20.

19. James Cone, *The Spiritual and the Blues* (Maryknoll, NY, Orbis, 1972).

20. Carol Tomlin, *Black Preaching Style*, Unpublished conference paper (1992).

21. Stuart Hall, 'Religious ideologies and social movements in Jamaica', in Robert Bocock and Kenneth Thompson, *Religion and Ideology*, (Manchester, Manchester University Press, 1985), p. 276.

22. The gospel genre is multiple in meaning (see Introduction). For many Black Christians, it is both spiritual and political:

Press along saints, press along in God's own way
Press along saints, press along in God's own way
Persecution we must face, trial and crosses in our way
But the hotter the battle, the sweeter the victory.

When many Black Christians sing this chorus, they express both an eschatological and existential reality, as shown, for example, in the militaristic emphases of the chorus. I would contend that when Black people sing about the 'battle' they refer not only to spiritual forms of struggle but also to the struggle for authentic existence as Black people. Similarly, when they sing of the 'victory', they refer not only to the imminent return of Christ but also to the realisation that it is possible to press along despite the dehumanising forces unleashed against the Black community. This point is well illustrated by the many occasions when things go wrong in the Black community, and the Church responds by asking someone to 'raise a chorus'. Here, raising a chorus is an act of defiance, and a form of cultural resistance.

23. The body plays an important role in the articulation of resistance. As mentioned by Hall, in Black expressive cultures the body is a canvas. An equivalent in the Black Church is the issue of 'dressing-up' for Sunday. Although it is important to be critical of materialism in Black Churches, and of the often extraordinary lengths travelled for the sake of looking good, there is also something positive in Black Church dress. In a context of Black dehumanisation, through negative representation of Black people in White popular culture, Black dress-styles permit Black Christians to express their 'somebodyness' through a visual aesthetic. Black dress-styles in the Church are a counter-statement which affirm the Black body and Black style. Here, to 'give of your best to God' means not only to do good but to look good: aesthetics are given ontological significance. In *In Search of Our Mother's Garden*, Alice Walker argues that the desire for freedom and resistance to oppression is historically expressed in the production of domestic art. Domestic art is whatever you can get your hands on to create self-worth. Likewise, in the traditions of the Black Church, dress has been used as a similar form of creative expression and cultural resistance.

24. See Paul Gilroy, *There Ain't No Black in the Union Jack*, pp. 197–209.

25. Ferdinand de Saussure, *A Course in General Linguistics*, trans. W. Baskin (New York, McGraw Hill, 1966).

26. Carl Jung, *Man and His Symbols* (New York, Dell, 1968).

27. Paul Tillich, *Dynamics of Faith* (New York, Harper Colophon Books, 1957).

28. J. L. Segundo, *The Liberation of Theology* (Maryknoll, NY, Orbis, 1970).

Chapter 8   Sisters in the house: the emergence and challenge of womanist theology in Britain

1. See, for example, Roswith Gerloff, *A Plea for Black British Theologies: the Black Church Movement in Britain in its Transatlantic Cultural and Theological Interaction*, Vol. 1 (Frankfurt, Peter Lang, 1992); also, Iain Macrobert, *Black Pentecostalism, its Origins, Functions and Theology*, Unpublished PhD Thesis (University of Birmingham, 1989).

2. For example, see Scholars Press series: Katie G. Cannon, *Black*

Womanist Ethics (Atlanta, Georgia, Scholars Press, 1988); Emile M. Townes, *Womanist Justice, Womanist Hope* (Atlanta, Georgia, Scholars Press, 1993); and Jacquelyn Grant, *White Woman's Christ, Black Women's Jesus: Feminist Christology and Womanist Response* (Atlanta, Georgia, Scholars Press, 1989).

3. See Delores Williams, *Sisters in the Wilderness: The Challenge of Womanist God-Talk* (Maryknoll, Orbis Press, 1993); also, Renita Weems, *Just a Sister Away: A Womanist Vision of Women's Relationships in the Bible* (San Diego, California, LauraMedia, 1988).

4. Victor Anderson, *Beyond Ontological Blackness* (New York, Continuum, 1995).

5. Patricia Hill Collins, *Black Feminist Thought, Knowledge, Consciousness and the Politics of Empowerment* (London, Routledge, 1990), pp. 201ff.

6. See James Cone, *God of the Oppressed* (Maryknoll, NY, Orbis, 1974).

7. See Kelly Brown Douglas, *The Black Christ* (Maryknoll, Orbis, 1994).

8. Jacquelyn Grant, *White Woman's Christ, Black Women's Jesus: Feminist Christology and Womanist Response* (Atlanta, Georgia, Scholars Press, 1989).

9. Hazel V. Carby, 'White woman listen! Black feminism and the boundaries of sisterhood', in Centre for Contemporary Cultural Studies, *The Empire Strikes Back: Race and Racism in 70s Britain* (London, Routledge, 1982).

10. See Cone and Wilmore (eds), op. cit.

11. Kelly Brown Douglas, *The Black Christ*, p. 79.

12. ibid., p. 98.

13. Elaine Foster, 'Women and the inverted pyramid of the Black Churches in Britain', in Gita Sahgal and Nira Yuval-Davis (eds), *Refusing Holy Orders: Women and Fundamentalism in Britain* (London, Virago Press, 1992).

14. ibid.

15. See Jacquelyn Grant, 'Womanist Jesus and the mutual struggle for liberation', in Randall Bailey and Jacquelyn Grant (eds), *The Recovery of Black Presence* (Nashville, Abingdon Press, 1995).

16. While this group is not the first generation of womanists – womanist sensibilities and perspectives can be found in the first generation of immigrants from the Caribbean – they are the first generation to have used texts as a tool of liberation.

17. Elaine Foster, 'Women and the inverted pyramid of the Black Churches in Britain'.

18. Eve Pitts, 'Black womanist ethics' in Paul Grant and Raj Patel (eds), *A Time to Speak: Perspectives of Black Christians in Britain*, (Nottingham, Russell Press, 1990).

19. See Ann Loades (ed.), *Feminist Theology: A Reader* (London, SPCK, 1990).

20. Jill Brown is currently a part-time MPhil/PhD research student at Birmingham University, and church worker at Saltley Methodist Church in Birmingham.

21. Kate Coleman is a PhD student at Birmingham University and also an ordained Baptist minister.

22. Novette Thompson is a PhD student at Birmingham University and an ordained Methodist minister.

23. Valentina Alexander was the first African–Caribbean person to complete a PhD on the Black Church in Britain (Warwick University, 1997). She is currently lecturing in London.

24. See Valentina Alexander, 'How a Black woman in Britain returns to her spiritual rites', (unpublished conference paper, 1997).

25. Michelle Campbell is an MPhil/PhD student at Birmingham University.

26. For example, *Black British Feminism* (Routledge, 1997) by Heidi Safia Mirza, has nothing to say on Black women and the Church.

Chapter 9   Forgive and forget? a Black Christian political rereading of the Lord's Prayer

1. See John Wilkinson, *The Church in Black and White* (St Andrews Press, 1994).

2. See 'The Bible and culture collective', *The Post-Modern Bible* (Yale University Press, 1995), p. 35.

3. For a good discussion of contemporary debates see, 'The Bible and culture collective'.

4. Iain Macrobert, *Black Pentecostalism, its Origins, Functions and Theology*, Unpublished PhD Thesis (University of Birmingham, 1989).

5. See Theo Smith, *Conjuring Culture, Biblical Formations of Black America* (NY and London, Oxford University Press, 1994).

6. See James Cone and Gayraud Wilmore (eds), *Black Theology and Documentary History, 1979–1992*, Vol. 2 (Maryknoll, Orbis, 1992).
7. Earlier in this volume I mention the theological significance of the concept of Dread.
8. Horace Campbell, *Rasta and Resistance*, pp. 22–3.
9. See Valentina Alexander, *Breaks Every Fetter?*, PhD dissertation (University of Warwick, 1997).
10. Robert Hood makes the claim that Rasta was the Caribbean's first liberation theology. See Robert Hood, *Must God remain Greek*, p. 87ff.
11. Lewin Williams, *Caribbean Theology* (Frankfurt, Peter Lang), p. 17.
12. Valentina Alexander, *Breaks Every Fetter*.
13. See Jill Brown, MA dissertation (Selly Oak College, 1997).
14. Comel West, *Prophetic Fragments* (Trenton NY, Africa World Press Eerdmans, 1988).
15. See Dwight Hopkins, *Shoes that Fit our Feet, Sources for a Constructive Black Theology* (Maryknoll, NY, Orbis, 1993).
16. See Kortright Davis, *Emancipation Still Comin', Explorations in Caribbean Emancipatory Theology* (Maryknoll, NY, Orbis, 1990).
17. Franz Fanon, *The Wretched of the Earth* (London, Penguin Books, 1990).
18. Kelly Brown Douglas, *The Black Christ* (Maryknoll, NY, Orbis, 1994).